RACING CARS
RACING CARS
RACING CARS
RACING CARS

RACING CARS

RACING CARS
RACING CARS
RACING CARS

by Richard Hough
with an introduction by Jim Clark

Paul Hamlyn·London

Designed by Clare Osborn
Published by PAUL HAMLYN LTD
Drury House · Russell Street · London WC2
© Copyright 1966 Paul Hamlyn Ltd

Printed in Czechoslovakia by TSNP, Martin

Contents

Introduction

To the enthusiast there can never be too many books about motor racing. Dedicated motoring fans will be absorbed by the exciting descriptions of classic motor races that Richard Hough has provided in *Racing Cars*.

Readers will be as fascinated as I am with the wealth of historical detail given in this book. And the discussion of the relative merits of the different racing marques will not only be of interest to a great many readers but will spark off argument in many motor clubrooms!

Richard Hough has devoted considerable space to explaining the difference between American track racing and the European-style Grand Prix. Now that the two types of racing have moved so much closer to each other, when car designs are becoming more similar, and since there is some discussion of the possibility of Indianapolis-style and Grand Prix cars racing on a directly competitive basis (as far as engine size is concerned), the publication of *Racing Cars* is timely.

While there is still some bitterness about the new Grand Prix formula, the pros and cons of matching European and American cars will no doubt be debated for some time to come.

Having driven a car built for Indianapolis (on test) on a road circuit, I can say with some conviction that closer liaison between American and European race organizers is practicable. Obviously, further modifications to regulations will be necessary by both parties, but the American acceptance of rear-engined cars after years of design stagnation is a major step towards closer co-operation.

In this connection I would commend to younger readers in particular Richard Hough's discussion of the attempts by drivers such as Jack Brabham to break into American track racing with Grand Prix cars. The fact that the Indianapolis classic was dominated by European cars in its early years, and that there were several successful European cars running at Indy at different times during its more recent history, is often forgotten amid the very gratifying reportage of the recent Lotus and Ford visits to the Brickyard in 1963, 1964 and 1965.

It is worth mentioning that readers whose motoring history is a trifle vague will find out how much co-operation there was between European and American motor racing interests during the early days of the sport.

To speculate on the future of motor racing, both as a spectator and participant sport, in the light of its truly international appeal, is an interesting pastime. One development I believe is inevitable: European constructors of Grand Prix cars will have to face up to severe competition from countries comparatively new to the sport (as they have already had to do in sports car racing). In the same way American track racers have had to completely rethink their approach to car construction, after European entry into races like Indianapolis.

Giants in the Dust

1895

1. The first-ever motor race. Here is M. Levassor's Panhard, triumphant in the Paris-Bordeaux-Paris, a 732-mile epic

2. The great Frenchman averaged 14.91 m. p. h. in this race, a good fast trot as can be seen from the spectators hurrying alongside

1 You would have to be over seventy-five years old, and have a good memory, to remember the first motor race. If you are around ninety today you might have driven in it.

The motor-car became a practical, workable proposition in the 1890's. The first ever motor race was in 1895. The average speed was only 15 m.p.h., the pace of a four-minute-miler. But the race was a long one of 732 miles, run over dusty, pot-holed, stone-strewn roads no better than farm tracks, and through narrow village streets and over high hills. The cars were primitive horseless carriages almost without springs, with wooden solid-tyred wheels, powered by crude engines of around 5 h.p.

The winner of this race from Paris to Bordeaux and back was Emile Levassor, one of the handful of enthusiastic Frenchmen who made their country the leading manufacturer of automobiles in the early days. His car was a Panhard of 2 cylinders (just like the sporty little Panhards of today!), but the engine was of German design and built under licence.

The German pioneers of the internal combustion engine were Wilhelm Maybach and Gottlieb Daimler, who worked together and designed the Daimler engine that won that first race for Panhard et Levassor; and Karl Benz, a brilliant engineer of humble origin who was building cars — and selling them — in the 1880's.

Another great name of those early days was Peugeot.

2 A Peugeot was second to the Panhard in the Bordeaux race, even if it was *six hours* behind the winner. Then there was Amédée Bollée, who built nippy little three-wheelers, one of which covered 60 kilometres in an hour in 1896. The Bollées were responsible for the start of the *voiturette,* or small car, which has raced in numerous forms right up to Formula III racing today. *Voiturettes* have exercised the skill of designers for nearly seventy years, as well as providing a form of training school for racing drivers.

In spite of the successful Bollées and the small Renaults, racing cars continued to grow in size. There was no regulation limiting engine capacity, and designers found that the bigger the engine, the greater the power and the higher the speed. It was as simple as that. The Panhard of just over 1 litre which had won the Paris-Bordeaux-Paris race quickly grew to double this capacity, then to $4\frac{1}{2}$ litres, and by 1900 the racing Panhard was powered by an engine of over 7 litres, which gave out some 30 h.p. The Mors of the same year — and this was to prove a very successful racing name — had an engine of 10 litres.

These early racing cars were crude and brutish. A Grand Prix driver of today taking over the controls of an 1899 Panhard could be forgiven if he mistook his mount for a rather fast, and highly dangerous, traction engine. The vast engine — three times the capacity of the 1966 Formula I engine — turned over slowly and sounded like a hesitant Maxim gun. Every explosion shook the simple wooden chassis and sent a shock wave up the steering column to the driver's hands on the tiller. There was no throttle as we know it today. The engine normally turned over at a constant speed, being controlled by the quadrant-change gears, the primitive brake, the decelerator when one was fitted, and, to a limited degree, by the ignition control. The handling of these cars at touring speeds demanded at once finesse, sharp timing and Herculean strength. To drive a 10 litre Mors from Paris to Toulouse at an average of over 40 m.p.h. called for near superhuman qualities, and real nippiness at repairing punctures.

Apart from a great increase in engine size, and the introduction of pneumatic tyres, electric ignition, new metals and other advances, the first five years of motor racing had demonstrated little real technical progress in the refinement of the internal combustion engine, the transmission of its power to the driving wheels, and the chassis. The year 1901, however, marked a real turning point in the progress of development of the motor-car, and consequently of the racing car.

From their earliest days many motor-car manufacturers had used German-designed Daimler engines to power their automobiles. The Daimler car itself was also highly regarded. The 1901 model brought the company new fame, and quite outshone anything available from its rivals in France, Italy and Britain. The 35 h.p. car possessed a frame of channel steel in place of wood, and a gate gear-change similar in principle to manual gearboxes in common use to this day, in place of the clumsy and noisy quadrant gear-change. Steering by wheel instead of by tiller was introduced.

Instead of a bent pipe, a new type of honeycomb radiator kept down the working temperature of the motor more effectively. The engine, too, greatly refined, revealed features which increased its efficiency, such as a low-tension magneto ignition, and a manual operation of the degree of lift of the inlet valves. This last controlled the intake of gas to the combustion

1900

3. The Automobile Club's 1,000 Miles Trial, May 1900 'An undertaking great and unprecedented in this country, which by its success from start to finish has accomplished marvels in forwarding the interests of automobilism in this realm.' So wrote a contemporary reporter. Here is Frank Hedges Butler (Panhard) on the last leg passing through St Albans

3

chamber, and thus provided the driver with overriding control of the engine speed. Further to emphasize the revolutionary nature of their car, the Daimler company gave it a new name. Mercedes was the beloved daughter of one of the company's most influential salesmen in France, Emile Jellinek (he was also a banker, socialite and diplomat). Everyone thought Mercedes was a good name — much better than Daimler, which was so very Teutonic. (The French had not greatly loved the Germans since their country had been invaded and their capital besieged by them thirty years earlier.)

The 35 h.p. Mercedes of 1901 is commonly regarded as the 'first modern car'. It deserves the title. Many of its features were not 'firsts'; but the shrewd employment of so many of them in one machine was altogether revolutionary. It was also at once considered very 'sporty', and racing versions of the car, with enlarged engines, followed. These were the famed Mercedes 60 and 90.

Besides the 60 and 90 Mercedes, other great names in motor racing in the first years of the new century were Panhard, Mors, Darracq and Richard Brasier from France, Itala and F.I.A.T. from Italy, and — at last — from Britain the fine Napier. The races were long and arduous, and were run over open roads from city to city — sometimes from one country to another, with controlled speed restrictions through the larger towns.

They ran from Paris to Berlin, from Paris to Vienna, and sometimes from Paris to Amsterdam and back. The distances were enormous, and so were the hazards when the great, high machines, powered by engines of more than 12-litres capacity, swept along the narrow roads, between tightly packed spectators lining the banks and cheering on their heroes. These giants who trailed their dust clouds across Europe were men like the Italian Felice Nazzaro, the French nobleman Chevalier René de Knyff, Henri Fournier, Christian Werner, S. F. Edge, Louis Wagner — brave and muscular men all, the twentieth century counterparts of the Roman charioteers of old.

These hazardous, hectic contests over the primitive roads of Europe culminated in the Paris-Madrid event of 1903. It was said that three million people turned out to watch, to pack the verges of the roads, sometimes to stroll into the middle of them in their eagerness to catch sight of the approach of the racing cars. For a few of them it was to end in death, for all of them it was the last opportunity to witness the nation-to-nation marathons that formed the heart of motor racing in its earliest and most stirring form. For the 1903 Paris—Madrid race was such a holocaust, such a tumultuous shambles, that it led to every European nation banning long-distance open road motor racing from city to city.

There were 216 entrants (and another 49 on motor bicycles) for this great race, the cars ranging from a De Boisse of 6 h.p. to 70 h.p. Panhards and Mors and half a dozen 90 h.p. Mercedes. There had never before been such a gathering of racing machinery.

This is how one eye-witness described the dawn start from Versailles of the British favourite, Charles Jarrott:

At five and twenty minutes to four the loud report of a bomb intimated that the officials were about to take action.

The engines of the first half dozen cars were now running, and while the din of the buzzing monsters was almost deafening, the blue haze of burnt lubricating oil rose up in huge volumes, poisoning the morning air. One of the officials scribbled something on a card, and, lifting the lid of the tea-caddy shaped metal box affixed to the side of the De Dietrich, asked Jarrott to get ready. The cool hand settled himself, his mechanician took his seat, and the first speed was slipped in. The voice of the official timekeeper was heard through the exhausts of the many engines; but the crowd had ceased to shout and whistle and sing. There was a tenseness in the air, and high above a lark's song as he mounted heavenward came down clearly to the earth. 'Dix', cried the timekeeper, 'Cinq, quatre,

4. *Emil Jellinek, diplomat, car dealer, and patron of the horseless carriage, whose daughter gave her name, Mercedes, to Herr Daimler's products*

1901
5. *This 40 h. p. 1901 model Mercedes set new standards*

1903-1904
6. *Napier, one of the greatest British names in 1904. Mark Mayhew at the helm*

7. *French Darracq, stripped for combat — and breaking the record*

8. *Jetnazy's 60 h.p. Mercedes, winner in the 1903 Gordon Bennett race held in Ireland*

9. *Same race, less successful 4-cylinder Winton Special contestant*

1903

10. *The Gordon Bennett. Baron de Caters, Mercedes. The Baroness sat in the front row of the grandstand, and every time her husband passed he would nod, amid spectators' cheers*

12. *Paris-Madrid, terminated at Bordeaux after the infamous holocaust, when the winner — shown here — was announced as Gabriel on his mighty Mors. What an epic!*

1904

11. *Circuit des Ardennes. Heath's Panhard*

13. *S. F. Edge, famous publicist, motorist and promoter of the wares of the Napier Company*

14. *France, lacking a closed track like Brooklands, continued to run races on closed public roads*

trois, deux — *partez!*' In went the clutch, and with a wave of his hand in response to the cries '*Bonne chance! A Bordeaux!* Good luck, old man!' Jarrott sped away on his De Dietrich, opening the Paris–Madrid race, which fate had already decreed should have no end.

Some nine hours later the first car was seen as a black dot within a vast cloud of its own dust, tearing towards the Bordeaux control point. Between dawn and dusk of that hot day in May 1903 occurred acts of gallantry and foolishness, incidents of skill in over-taking on narrow roads in thick dust-clouds, of tragedy as dogs and errant spectators were knocked down or drivers crashed in their efforts to avoid them. The death toll was never announced. But among the dead drivers were Marcel Renault of France, and the equally popular Loraine Barrow of Britain.

When news of the tragedies reached Paris, the Minister of the Interior (whose poor control of the race was the main cause of the fiasco) prohibited it from continuing, and the Spanish authorities followed suit. So the leader at Bordeaux turned out to be the winner of the last of the 'dust and glory' classics. At the time the magnitude of Gabriel's achievement in aver-aging 65.3 m.p.h. on his Mors was forgotten amid the outcry and outrage, the laments and accusations, that followed. It is remembered today as one of the epics of motor racing history.

2474 A ROTARY PHOTO E.C.   MR S F EDGE.   FOULSHAM & BANFIELD

ON HIS 6 CYLINDER "NAPIER CAR" ON THE BROOKLANDS TRACK.

15

16

17

14

Three of the great pioneers

15. *Karl Benz*
16. *Wilhelm Maybach*
18. *Gottlieb Daimler*

17. 19. *Two shots of the mighty leviathan, 1904 90 h.p. Mercedes. Jenatzy and Baron de Caters are among those in silent admiration*

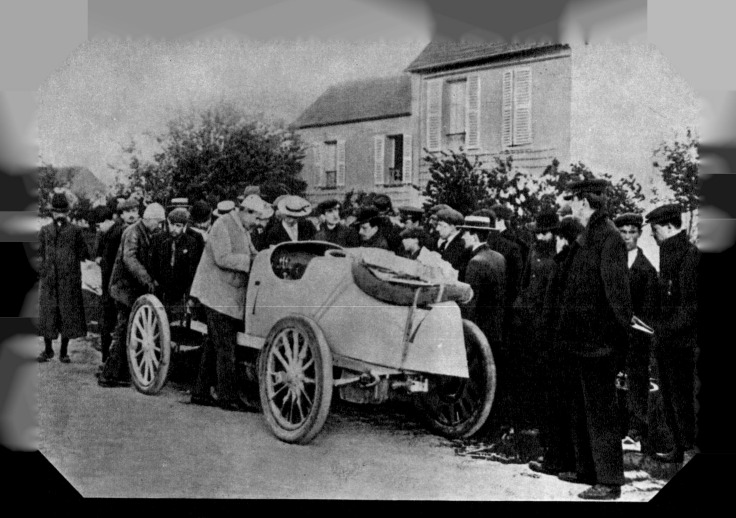

Paris-Madrid race 1903

20. An album of the last-ever dust-and-glory, city-to-city races, when over-enthusiastic spectators and drivers alike caused a large number — no one ever seems to have counted — of injuries and deaths. Here is Fournier coping with ignition troubles near Rambouillet

22. The Englishman Charles Jarrott thundering up to the finishing line at Bordeaux

23. And here are more survivors — Baron de Crawhez, 90 h.p. Panhard

21. Marcel Renault with the 30 h.p. car carrying his name, in which he was to be killed

24. Jenatzy with his vast 90 h.p. Mercedes

25. Louis Renault's 30 h.p. Seconds later he was in tears on hearing the news of his brother's death

The Coming of Science

Two wealthy Americans played a large part in Edwardian motor racing. One was William K. Vanderbilt, Jr, a multimillionaire, a sportsman, and also a skilful and muscular racing driver. There will be more about him later. The other was James Gordon Bennett, the newspaper proprietor and great supporter of amateur sport — balloon, aircraft and motor-boat racing as well as car racing.

From 1900 to 1905 an annual event for the Gordon Bennett cup was run on open roads or closed circuits in Europe. A Napier driven by S. F. Edge was the winner of the Paris—Innsbruck event in 1902, the first notable British motor racing success. The following year it was run in Ireland, Jenatzy's Mercedes 60 triumphing. By then it had become an international event of great importance, and the last two Gordon Bennetts were so hotly contested by factory sponsored teams that Gordon Bennett considered the amateur element could no longer be sustained. His withdrawal of the Cup caused the Automobile Club de France, which existed mainly to support the growing French automobile industry, to organize the first of its Grands Prix.

Grand Prix racing as we know it today stemmed from this race at Le Mans in 1906, for which there were entered twenty-six French cars, six cars from Italy and three from Germany. Gigantism was still the order of the day. The Panhards were of 18 litres capacity, and few of the engines were of less than 12 litres. The race consisted of three laps of 65 miles each on two successive days on a closed circuit. Preparations went on for weeks before the race. Bridges were built across the road, enclosures marked off at the corners, and twin tunnels connected the pits on the outside of the circuit with the great gaily decorated grandstand opposite. 'The race,' wrote a reporter, 'was one of men, luck, and tyres, chiefly tyres...' Stones, dust, chemicals and melted tar also played their part, and a special eye doctor was kept busy extracting foreign objects from the eyes of the heroic drivers. One of the chief sufferers was Jenatzy, probably

1898

Plate 1. Paris-Amsterdam-Paris, 889 miles. The great Panhard driver Charron pulls out to pass a Bollée

1901

Plate 2. Paris-Berlin. Fournier defeated all the Panhards, his Mors averaging 44.1 m.p.h. for the 687 miles

1902

Plate 3. Early British driver's success. Charles Jarrott wins the Circuit des Ardennes in 1902, with a broken front transverse spring, at 54 m.p.h. for the 318 miles. The car is a Panhard '70'

1906 French Grand Prix

26—29. The era of the big bangers, before the scientists and the metallurgists stepped in. This is the 1906 Grand Prix, the first in the classic series. From top to bottom: de la Touloubre, Clement-Bayard; Jenatzy, Mercedes; Lancia depot stop (dug-out pits were to come later); Szisz's winning Renau t. He averaged a remarkable 63 m.p.h.

Plate 4. The last Gordon Bennett, 1904. Théry's Richard-Brasier has just passed Charles Rolls's Wolseley

Plates 5. 6. The first Grand Prix, 1906. Szisz's Renault flashes by to victory. Szisz's race average of 63 m.p.h. was maintained largely thanks to his detachable rims

1904—1908

Plate 7. Mercedes's first Grand Prix victory, 1908. On the Dieppe circuit Lautenschlager averaged 68.9 m.p.h.

Plate 8.   3 litre 'voiturettes' at Boulogne, 1911. Bablot's Delage (10) finally defeated Boillot's 2-cylinder Peugeot

Plate 9.   1912. The giant vanquished. Boillot's Peugeot challenges the vast red F.I.A.T.

1907

30.   Targa Florio. Felice Nazzaro's winning FIAT

1908

31.   'When men were men . . .' And motors were motors. Frank Newton's Napier at Saltburn

MR F NEWTON ON 90 HP NAPIER

102 MLS PER HOUR SALTBURN SANDS JUNE 27 1908.

1910

32. Ushering in a new age, the 1910 Hispano-Suiza which set new standards of efficiency. The name derives from the Spanish-Swiss origins of this esteemed and long-lived make. The designer was Swiss engineer Marc Birkigt, who worked in Barcelona. The King of Spain (Alfonso) lent his name to the model, before a French-based factory was set up

1912

33. The epochal pioneer work of Ernst Henri (another Swiss) was manifested in the Peugeot Grand Prix car, winner of Grands Prix and at Indianapolis

the fastest man there. It was left to the Hungarian ace, Szisz, to come through, unscarred, as the winner in his massive Renault. Felice Nazzaro of Italy ran second in his F. I. A. T. (or Fiat, as it became after 1906). He avenged his defeat the following year when the second Grand Prix was held on a circuit at Dieppe. His winning speed was 70.5 m.p.h. Germany's turn came in 1908, when Mercedes and Benz cars swept the board.

These foreign successes were too much for the French. The point of the Grand Prix was to provide publicity for the speed and durability of French cars. They were scarcely succeeding in their aim. Motor racing continued, on a minor note, elsewhere, but there was no Grand Prix of the Automobile Club de France in 1909, 1910 or 1911.

Until 1907 there had been few technical advances beyond those originated by the 35 h.p. Mercedes of 1901, and many manufacturers were slow to imitate the most advanced features of this car. Speed was still acquired by four great thundering pistons that took their time going up and down. But by 1908, and the last of the Edwardian Grands Prix, designers — and especially German designers — were beginning to have new thoughts on the future shape of the racing car. Engines with inclined valves and even with overhead

camshafts made their appearance, and there was a marked reduction in capacity. Yet almost half the cars were timed at 100 m.p.h. or more on one of the straights.

Was the future of racing car engine design to be found in more science and fewer litres? A number of engineers thought so. And they had a four year lull in which to prove their case.

Since the beginning of automobile racing, technical advances have been accomplished in a series of sudden revolutions, followed by periods of maintaining the *status quo*. Perhaps the most important of these revolutions occurred between 1908 and 1914. During these

six years some of the greatest designers the world has known made their mark. The results of their endeavours can be found in some form or another in every production and racing car built over the past fifty years.

The greatest of these engineers were Ernest Henri and Marc Birkigt from Switzerland, Ettore Bugatti from Italy, Ferdinand Porsche from Austria, Paul Daimler (Gottlieb's son) and Fritz Nallinger from Germany. Others to make notable contributions were Laurence Pomeroy of the Vauxhall company in Britain, while in America the Duesenberg brothers, Fred and August, revealed the first fruits of their genius.

There is no space here to discuss the work in detail

of all these great figures. Undoubtedly the most influential racing car designer of all time was Ernest Henri. Today we know the Peugeot as a rather staid and conservative French family motor-car. From 1912 Peugeot racing cars, constructed from the designs of Ernest Henri, were the most feared and the most successful in Europe and America.

When Ernest Henri, a young man of only twenty-seven, was commissioned to build a new Grand Prix racing car by Robert Peugeot in 1911, he started with a clean sheet of paper on his board. With the co-operation of Peugeot's three leading drivers, Georges Boillot, Jules Goux and Paul Zuccarelli, he had com-

1911

34. Another product of genius, that was to flower until the Second World War. Ettore Bugatti's 16-valve Type 13 machine at the start of the Grand Prix de France at Le Mans in 1911

1912

35. British engineering talent was notably revealed in Laurence H. Pomeroy's 'Prince Henry' Vauxhall, here seen in the 1912 Swedish Trials

pleted within a few months the detailed specification for the most epochal racing car of all time. The engine had a modest capacity of 7.6 litres, a mere 'mini' among the thunderers from Panhard and Fiat and Lorraine-Dietrich. But radical ingenuity more than offset this litre-handicap. High piston speed was sought above all else, and was achieved by the use for the first time of two shaft-driven overhead camshafts, operating four valves for each of the 4 cylinders. The valves were inclined in the hemispherical combustion chambers at 45 degrees. Inclined and multiple valves were not entirely new. Nor was the overhead camshaft directly operating the valves. Ettore Bugatti, among others, had already made experiments in the same direction. But like so much else of Peugeot's overall design, in the engine department there was manifested a blend of the new with features from earlier designs that had proved their efficiency and showed promise of fruitful development. Considerable ingenuity was shown also in the design of the Grand Prix Peugeot's chassis. So that, although the car was scarcely faster than the 1908 monsters, it achieved its power with less weight, and was altogether more manageable.

At the revived Grand Prix at Dieppe in 1912 it took the honours at its first outing. At Indianapolis the following year it lapped the brickyard at 93.5 m.p.h. and again proved the winner.

This was the largest of the racing Peugeots. Smaller and improved versions of the same basic design brought the company further successes over the following years.

To witness one of these, we must go to Boulogne in the early autumn of 1913. Here on a rough, twisting, hilly circuit, inland east of the town, seventeen racing cars, including a pair of Buicks from America, and Vauxhalls and Sunbeams from Britain, and a team of three Peugeots, struggled for more than six hours for the Coupe de l'Auto. The intention of the promoters was to encourage the development of smaller-engined cars, and the capacity was limited to 3 litres. The Peugeots, neat, light, stocky little cars, were to be driven by Goux, Boillot and Rigal, and were hot favourites from the start. Henri had produced a scaled-down version of his Grand Prix car, using the same engine layout, but modifying the valve angle from 45 to 60 degrees, employing a train of gears to drive the camshafts and raising the compression ratio, so that the output of 90 h.p. at 3,000 r.p.m. was about the same as that of the earlier big car. In 1912, the British Sunbeams with side-valve engines had taken with ease the first three places in the Coupe de l'Auto. Robert Peugeot was determined that France should not again be humiliated in this way.

The cars were started off singly at timed intervals — the custom at that time. 'Suddenly one engine howls louder than all the others, there is a snick from the gear-lever, and at the fall of the starter's hand two

1913 Coupe de l'Auto

36. 37. Now the age of science had really arrived, and every machine bore evidence of fresh engineering consideration. Above: before the start, the winning 3 litre Peugeots, and, behind, Coatalen's Sunbeams, one of which came in third. Below: Watson on one of Pomeroy's Vauxhalls, in earnest conversation with his mechanic. Note two spare wheels — one studded and one grooved

38. 1913 Coupe de l'Auto — continued: Lee Guiness's Sunbeam, highest placed British car

39. Rigal's Peugeot at Bamethun. He came in fifth

40. Boillot's winning Peugeot

41. And the reason behind it all. Henri's twin overhead camshaft engine — 'the beginning of the modern racing engine'

huge fountains of road grit are flung backwards by the driving wheels . . .' One by one the cars disappear amid dust and flying stones towards La Capelle, while the crowds packed deep along the sides of the Boulogne streets await the arrival of their favourite, Georges Boillot.

The French driver Jean Chassagne driving a bright red Sunbeam is first to complete the lap; then A. J. Hancock's Vauxhall, a few hundred yards behind. Then, unexpectedly, an airplane — a rare sight indeed in those days — sweeps above the road, heralding the arrival of Boillot; who would soon be shot down while flying against the Germans. 'Above the fizzle of the Gnome comes the bleat of the trumpeter, and Boillot's blue Peugeot sweeps round the bend and disappears with a flash and a roar. This provides the first thrill of the day, for finely as its driver judges the bend there is more than a little skidding, although it is quickly and masterfully corrected.' He has lapped at least two minutes faster than either of the British cars. On his next appearance, he goes even wider, and sends the spectators scattering.

The sun blazes down. The dust settles ever more thickly in the windless air. The gaps between the arrival and screaming departure from the corners becomes wider as car after car falls out. Neither Buick survives the third lap. An F.A.B. and a Zenia fall

out, and there are halts by the roadside and at the pits to change wheels as sharp stones tear through the tyre covers. Guinness (of the brewing family) holds on, four minutes behind Boillot after two-and-a-half hours' racing. But neither he nor his team-mate Chassagne can hope to match their Sunbeams against the light 95 m.p.h. Peugeots, though Guinness gets ahead of Goux after a slow pit stop by the Frenchman, and actually holds this place for four laps — a tremendous achievement. Then Goux puts his foot hard down. The Peugeot magnificently meets the demands of its driver. Skidding wide at every corner, and then accelerating with wheelspin, and up through the close ratio gears (there isn't much power from the Henri engine at under 2,000 r. p. m.), through Desvres, up through the Haute Forêt, along the straight flat out to Wirwignes ... A lap in under thirty minutes, the only one of the race. And Guinness is left behind, to take a fine third behind the triumphant Peugeots.

For 1914 the Grand Prix regulations limited engine size to $4\frac{1}{2}$ litres. Perhaps this was the greatest Grand Prix of all time. Every motor manufacturing nation except America was represented: fourteen teams making forty-one cars in all. Almost all of them revealed the influence of the technical revolution wrought by Ernest Henri two years earlier. The engines of every car, except of one team, utilized the overhead

1914

42. 43. *After lying dormant since 1908, the Tourist Trophy was renewed in 1914, and was hotly contested by a wide range of British and Continental cars, although Peugeot and Mercedes were notable absentees. These are two of the most advanced British designs. Above: the Vauxhall, and Below: the Sunbeam, the winning make, and still raced today in the hands of its present owner*

44. 45. 46. *The 1914 Grand Prix marked an invasion of racing cars from Germany that was to be followed only weeks later by her less peacefully-intended army. Both campaigns were conducted with military discipline: the first succeeded, the latter finally failed. Here are the German Mercedes busily annihilating the French defenders*

camshaft for the operation of the valves, and ingenuity was shown in the construction of the chassis — four-wheel brakes for example — as well as under the bonnet. Mercedes was back, intent on repeating their 1908 triumph. The hopes of France rested on the Delages, and above all on Henri's new Peugeots. It was a ding-dong battle from start almost to the finish — a desperate Franco-German duel that presaged the grim, bloody struggle that was soon to break out between the two nations. At last Georges Boillot, the idol of the crowds, broke a valve on his car on the twentieth lap while going flat out after Lautenschlager's Mercedes. He had to be helped from his car, weeping . . .

For France it was a bitter end to a great era of motor racing.

Racing Comes to the U.S.A.

1906

47. 48. The Vanderbilt Cup Races on Long Island offered the Americans the opportunity to see road racing in the European manner. Above: Gabriel's de Dietrich. Below: Wagner winning the 1906 event

At the time when the Gordon Bennett Cup races were achieving their greatest success in Europe, William K. Vanderbilt Jr, the other American to play an important part in motor racing, offered a cup bearing his name to the winner of a motor race to be run on a public road circuit on Long Island in America.

Vanderbilt had not only witnessed the city-to-city racing in Europe; he had tasted its thrills at first hand as a driver — and no mean driver at that. His skill as the sponsor and organizer of the motor race were not so great, however, and the first three Vanderbilt Cup events were even more chaotic than the Paris-Madrid race that had signalled the end of open road racing in Europe. Local residents, and especially the farmers, resented the noisy racing cars and the thousands of thrill-seeking spectators from New York City who invaded the pastoral peace of Long Island. Nails and obstructions were placed on the road, to add to the hazards and the death toll.

Few people could agree with Vanderbilt's own comment on the first race that it was 'a good, clean contest, full of interest'; though interest was not lacking. On the other hand the multimillionaire-sportsman did succeed, in all three races, in luring over from Europe the greatest teams of the day. The Vanderbilt Cup events were supported by F.I.A.T. and Itala of Italy, Panhard, Lorraine-Dietrich and Darracq of France, Mercedes of Germany, among others, as well as by numerous American manufacturesrs. And many of the heroes of the European classics sailed the Atlantic to take part — Jenatzy, Lancia, Wagner, Nazzaro, Cagno, and many more. But it was left to George Heath of America, driving a giant Panhard, to take the honours in 1904, to the delight of the crowd, who swarmed on to the road after the first three cars had taken the flag, and abruptly halted the race. In 1905 Hemery's Darracq won at over 60 m.p.h. after a particularly bloody race of 283 miles. And the French Darracq triumphed again twelve months later, in the hands of Louis Wagner.

But this time the outcry against the annual 'blood

49. *A Vanderbilt Cup contestant in 1906 — 35 c.v. 4-cylinder Renault*

1911

50. *Indianapolis — soon to become the throbbing heart of American racing. The start of the first '500' with Case, Simplex, Interstate and National (right to left) on the front row*

50

bath' on Long Island was too powerful to resist, and Vanderbilt had to build a closed circuit on private land, the Long Island Motor Parkway. His Cup was raced for three more times on this private circuit, in 1908, 1909 and 1910. If anything these races were even more chaotic and casualty-ridden than the earlier events.

Meanwhile, board and dirt racing on oval and circular tracks had gained in popularity all over the United States. This was as remote from the European style of racing as a hundred yards sprint is from a cross-country marathon. But it was highly spectacular, and it packed in the crowds. In 1908 four businessmen from Indianapolis, then the most important centre of automobile manufacture in the country, decided to set up a 2½-mile test track just outside the city. It consisted of two straights of 3301 feet and two of 660 feet, connected by four shallow-banked turns of equal radius. The surface was of crushed stone and asphalt.

Short races were run on this track in 1909 and 1910, but they were not very successful. Drivers complained of the poor surface, and there were several deaths. By 1911 the promoters had to decide whether to abandon racing altogether, or improve the facilities. Thanks to their courage, one of the greatest sporting spectacles in the world has annually taken place at the 'Indy

51. And here is the first '500' winner in 1911. Ray Harroun's Marmon, which averaged 74.59 m.p.h. 'All the credit belongs to the Marmon company for building such a fine car. I never had the throttle wide open at any time,' remarked Harroun after it was all over

brickyard' ever since. They came to the wise decision to re-surface the entire track with millions of stone bricks (much later these were surfaced over again), and to run one race only every year, on Memorial Day, May 30th. And it was to be of 500 miles.

American cars dominated the first-ever Indianapolis, the winner being Ray Harroun on a Marmon Wasp at 74.59 m.p.h., or rather less than half the speed at which the 500 is run today.

By luck and skilful publicity the Indianapolis 500 captured the imagination of the American public. The crowds increased with the ballyhoo, and so did the prize money and the prestige from success at 'the World's Greatest Spectacle'. In 1913 the French and Italians — and some British too — came over in strength. They included a team of the ultra-advanced Peugeots, with Goux and Zuccarelli to drive them. The home side was represented by Stutz and Mercer — sporting dreams of American youth — and three Masons, with engines designed by Fred and August Duesenberg, who were later to create the status symbol of aspiring American millionaires. Indy tradition has it that Jules Goux's victory was achieved with the stimulus of no less than four bottles of champagne, taken in long drafts while wheels were changed. Certainly at the end his claim was that, 'Sans le bon vin, je n'aurais pas été en état d'être vainqueur!'

52. Number One Turn — Number One Race. Memorial Day, 1911. 5, Pope-Hartford, 8, Case, 9, Case

JOE DAWSON, WINNER 1912

JULES GOUX - 1913 WINNER.

The supremacy of France, if not of *le bon vin*, was upheld in 1914. Prize money was now over the 50,000 mark. Ettore Bugatti sent one of his new beautifully engineered single-camshaft 5 litre machines, with Ernest Friederich to drive. There was a 7 litre Excelsior from Belgium, a pair of $6\frac{1}{2}$ litre Delages, similar to the 1913 Grand Prix cars with all the overhead valves in line along the head. Two of Louis Coatalen's Sunbeams were sent from Britain, old Coupe de l'Auto cars with another 2 cylinders added to bring them up to $4\frac{1}{2}$ litres. And of course there was a strong contingent of Peugeots.

The Peugeots consisted of two factory-sponsored 5.6 litre cars, as used in the 1913 Grand Prix, to be driven by Goux and Boillot, and one of the Coupe de l'Auto machines of only 3 litres' capacity entered by French chocolate magnate Jacques Meunier, with Arthur Duray as driver.

This powerful line-up from Europe was faced by an American opposition consisting of Stutzs in the hands of Earl Cooper, Gil Anderson and that great champion, Barney Oldfield; Mercers, Burman Specials, Maxwells, and Duesenbergs in the hands of Eddie Rickenbacker and Willie Haupt. The 'Dusies' (Fred and August had now set up their own plant) were the only American cars which revealed any influence of the design sophistication evident in the French machines; the rest depended on thundering big engines — the Stutz had a swept volume of 7.4 litres.

The Peugeots were fastest in practice, Boillot getting within less than a mile an hour of the three-figure mark. But tyres were to be their undoing, as they have so often determined the Indy winner. For a brief moment one of the Mercers threatened French omnipotence; for the rest of the long and arduous race, run at record speed, the only question was 'Delage or Peugeot?' Would it be Thomas with his very fast Delage — or Duray, Goux or Boillot with the Peugeots? They were all driving on Palmer tyres, and there was little to choose between their speeds. But while the Delage lasted the race with only two tyre changes,

1912

53. Marmon was too busy building cars to meet orders resulting from his 1911 win to enter the next year

1913

54. Peugeot came, and saw, and conquered in 1913. Jules Goux completed the all-French triumph

1914

55. René Thomas makes it another French victory in 1914, this time for Delage

WINNER 1914
RENE THOMAS

the Peugeots were plagued with tyre failures caused by careless fitting and the pinching of the inner tubes. After numerous halts for changes, Boillot, racing magnificently three seconds behind the leader and with only a hundred miles to go, had a blow-out at speed. The French ace went into a huge skid down the straight, and overturned, luckily escaping injury. Duray then showed the real potential of the 'baby' Peugeot by beating all the American giants and taking second place, four minutes ahead of Guyot's second Delage.

Like the French Grands Prix of earlier days, the American classic seemed to be turning into a foreign benefit, despite all the efforts of the American designers. Stutz, Duesenberg and Maxwell (Mercer withdrew after engine failure) prepared steadfastly for the fray again in 1915.

For a time it seemed as if their efforts were going to be rewarded. The big Stutzs were in the first two places after eighty miles. Then their tyres began to let them down, and Dario Resta's Peugeot swept into first place, hotly pursued by Ralph DePalma in an independent Mercedes. These two fought tail-to-nose, nose-to-tail, for lap after lap, pushing the speed up higher than ever before. It was the most stirring combat the 500 had ever seen — France versus Germany, as in the Grand Prix of 1914; now once

56. *Vanderbilt Cup, Santa Monica, 1914. This is Grant on an Isotta-Fraschini*

1916

57. *Dario Resta's Peugeot*

1914

58. *What the crowds really came to see! Fifth International Grand Prix Race at Santa Monica, California, February 1914. A scene at Death Curve, named thus perhaps in expectation, for there had been no injuries before Marquis overdid it while in the lead with his Sunbeam on the 35th lap. 'The machine, when it stopped rolling, rested on the driver's body.'*

59. *DePalma, Mercedes, winning the 1914 Vanderbilt Cup*

60. *Another Death Curve episode. Pullen's Mercer was in the lead, too, when a detached wheel sent the crowds running. But his 7½ litre Mercer later won the Grand Prix which followed the Cup Race*

again, four thousand miles away across the Atlantic, the two nations were in bloody combat.

The lead changed time and again. Then, with 165 miles to go, the Peugeot's steering became erratic, and it was all Resta could do to hold the car on the turns. The gap widened to four minutes. Resta could do nothing. Three laps to go. It looked like a Mercedes victory . . . until suddenly a connecting rod broke, tore the crankcase and drained the engine of its oil.

Resta speeded up, the Mercedes limped on, a mechanical wreck, but with 3 cylinders still operating, almost without lubrication. To the credit of the rugged

German unit, it lasted out, lumbering along with a sickening, irregular beat. DePalma nursed it through those last miles, watching Resta gaining on him yard by yard. After an overall time of 5 hours, 33 minutes, 55 seconds — a record by a wide margin — the Mercedes took the flag. This was the first privately-entered victory since the series had begun.

Resta tried again with the Peugeot the following year — and this time triumphed by a wide margin. Then war closed down the gates of the Speedway; and Henri's Peugeot had to wait another three years before its third Memorial Day victory in 1919.

60

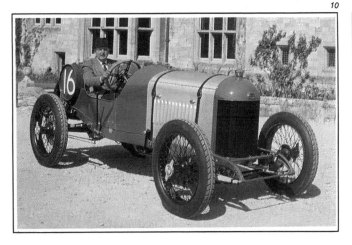

1913

Plates 10. 11. These beautifully restored pre-First World War racing cars can be seen at the Montagu Motor Museum, Beaulieu, England. Left: Delage. Right: Coupe de l'Auto Sunbeam. After their sweeping victory in 1912, Coatalen's sturdy and reliable cars could manage no better than third place behind the Peugeots in 1913

1911

Plate 12. Earlier Coupe de l'Auto Delage. Bablot averaged 54.8 m.p.h. on the Boulogne circuit, and defeated a formidable opposition of Peugeots, Sunbeams, Vauxhalls, Grégoires, Arrol-Johnstons and others

1921

Plate 13. *The technically advanced and painstakingly prepared Duesenbergs came to Le Mans for the first post-war Grand Prix, and one of the team cars driven by Jimmy Murphy scored America's first and only victory in a European Grand Prix*

1922

Plate 14. *First year of the 2 litre formula brought forth fascinating technical exercises fron Sunbeam, Rolland-Pilain, Ballot, Bugatti — and from Fiat, the winning make. Here is the veteran Nazzaro in his red 6-cylinder Fiat overtaking one of the 8-cylinder Bugattis*

America Invades France

1919
*61. New star, old name. Antonio Ascari victorious in S. 57/148
Fiat in Peggio di Berceto*

1920
*62. With the loss of Henri to Ballot, Peugeot withdrew from
racing, but earlier cars continued to appear in competition*
*63. After the First World War, Mercedes were soon back in
racing. This is the Sicilian Targa Florio circuit*

In Europe it is popularly believed that the Americans
have demonstrated little technical originality in their
racing cars. While it is true that there have been few
American racing automobile engineers of the calibre
of Ettore Bugatti or Ernest Henri, these few stand
out among the most brilliant in this specialized field.
The names of Fred and August Duesenberg, and of
Harry Miller, are enshrined for all time in the history
of the Indianapolis 500. But their influence spread
far beyond the brickyard; and in 1921 the Duesenberg
brothers brought off the biggest coup in American
racing history.

For the first and only time an American designed,
American built, American driven car won a European
Grand Prix — the French Grand Prix.

The war years had brought racing car development
to a temporary standstill. But during the same period
the airplane had grown up, maturing from the crude
and unreliable machine that had heralded the arrival
of Georges Boillot's Peugeot at the 1913 Coupe de
l'Auto to 150 m.p.h. fighters and massive four-engined
bombers designed to bomb Berlin from their French
bases. The life-or-death needs of fighting airmen had
resulted in a tremendous acceleration in the understanding of the internal combustion engine. One of
the lessons learnt by aero-engine designers was the
benefit to be derived from multi-cylinders. Successful

64. The beautifully prepared Duesenbergs before the start

65. André Boillot has his Talbot-Darracq topped up with water

66. Jules Goux's undersized Ballot which performed so bravely

67. Ralph DePalma (Ballot) and Mathis in his own 1½ litre are flagged away

68. Ballot and Duesenberg, last away, open their duel. Boyer (16) was soon to demonstrate the American car's superior torque

69. S. T. D. rivalry. Lee Guinness (Talbot number 4) tries to hold René Thomas's French Talbot-Darracq

racing cars before the First World War had been powered by 4 cylinder engines. But immediately after the 1918 Armistice the leading designers in Europe and in the United States began work on 8-cylinder in-line engines, which began a trend that was to endure for many years.

For the first post-war Grand Prix in 1921 the regulations (or Formula) decreed a limit in engine size of 3 litres. Germany was not allowed to take part; Italy withdrew her Fiats, and it looked as though it would be a French benefit and a dull event. However, a Franco-British entry of S.T.D. cars enlivened the list. S.T.D. (Sunbeam-Talbot-Darracq) was a motoring *entente cordiale* — although it was not always cordial — which for a number of years between the wars built cars in Britain and France. To everyone's confusion both racing and production cars were often identical except for their labels. The group's chief designer was Louis Coatalen, a great motor racing enthusiast, and an engineer noted more for his imitative than creative capacity.

The Talbots entered for the French Grand Prix were close copies of the French Ballots, designed by Ernest Henri. Peugeot had not officially raced since the war, and Monsieur Ballot, who had made a fortune building engines during the war, signed up Henri to design racing cars. These racing Ballots had already built up a reputation almost as fearsome as the pre-war Peugeots, winning many races in Europe and proving fastest at Indianapolis for three successive years, although victory had always eluded them in the United States, mainly through bad luck. Basically, they were similar in layout to Henri's Peugeots, with twin overhead camshafts and inclined valves, but through the influence of aero-engine design, and of Ettore Bugatti's aero-engines in particular, they had 8 cylinders in-line instead of 4.

In addition to these highly interesting straight-eight Anglo-French S.T.D. Talbots (or Talbot-Darracqs) and pure French Ballots, there appeared from America a full team of gleaming white, beautifully prepared Duesenbergs. The Duesenberg brothers were ascending towards the height of their racing fame. They had already made an impressive showing at Indianapolis, and the four machines they sent to France were the lightest of the 3 litre cars, very sturdy and reliable, and technically advanced. Under the influence of Indianapolis, with its four equally fast turns, they possessed only three-speed gearboxes, but the engines showed a remarkably high output over the whole speed range. And above all they had magnificent four-wheel brakes, far more effective than those of the French cars, operated by a mixture of glycerine and water.

The only other entries for the 1921 Grand Prix were a sports-type $1\frac{1}{2}$ litre Mathis and a 2 litre Ballot,

70. *Thomas again — worrying about his tyres?*

71. Aperitif *millionaire Dubonnet, fourth on his Duesenberg*

72. *Ralph DePalma's Ballot, despite a leaky tank, held on to second place*

70

71

72

both 4 cylinder machines that were given little chance of success.

The Grand Prix was to be fought out over a circuit that has since become famous as the home of the 24 Hours Le Mans sports car classic. Like Indianapolis, Le Mans was at that time an important car manufacturing centre, and the local automobile club has always been a highly active and successful one. In 1921, and up until 1929, the course ran right into the outskirts of the city itself, turning back to the south again at a diabolical hairpin at Pontlieue. Otherwise the road followed the same course at it does today, with the renowned Mulsanne straight and corner, the right-angled double twist at Tertre Rouge, and gentler double corner at White House. But in 1921 the road surface was no better than the *routes nationales* over which the Edwardian monsters had fought their way to Bordeaux and Toulouse. Dust was a constant hazard, and flying stones injured crews and damaged cars alike.

The cream of the world's drivers congregated at the Le Mans circuit in the heat of a marvellous summer to battle for victory at the first Grand Prix since the Franco-German epic of 1914. But this time France's main threat came from across the Atlantic. Moreover the Americans had sent their top drivers, Joe Boyer and Jimmy Murphy and Ralph DePalma, although the last of these was to drive for Ballot. All three Amer-

icans adjusted themselves with remarkable speed to the demands of road racing after American track racing, the twenty-seven year old Irish-American Murphy making a speciality of braking late and cutting through on the inside of Pontlieue and Mulsanne corners. Besides DePalma, the Ballots were in the hands of Jean Chassagne, Jules Goux and Louis Wagner, and Britain sent two of her top drivers, the Anglo-American Segrave and Lee Guinness for the Talbots.

The race was over thirty laps of the 10¾-mile circuit — a little over three hundred miles in all, and less than half the distance of the first Grand Prix at Le Mans fifteen years earlier. Yet this was a much more strenuous course, with great demands on brakes, and a real test of endurance. Above all there were the stones, spouting up from the rear wheels, a shrapnel-like deterrent to any would-be overtaker. The cars were started in pairs at thirty second intervals, first away being DePalma's Ballot and the little sports Mathis, which was soon left far behind by the 3 litre car.

There was little to choose between the speeds of the Ballots and Duesenbergs over the first few laps. DePalma completed the first lap in 8 minutes 16 seconds, as fast as any of the Duesenbergs. But the veteran Chassagne showed greater steadiness, and slowly pulled his way up through the field. Murphy

73. *Wagner's Ballot at White House Corner*

74. *Murphy's winning Duesenberg at the same corner*

75. *Segrave in for a wheel change*

76. *The winning Duesenberg takes the honours*

77. *Murphy after the cheers are over*

1921

78. Italian Grand Prix. Bordino on his Fiat 801

1922

79. French Grand Prix. De Viscaya with his Type 30 Bugatti

80. And here is Pietro Bordino in the same race with one of the 6-cylinder 2 litre Type 804 Fiats

led by less than two minutes after ten laps, and when he brought his white Duesenberg, now dusty and scarred by flying stones, into the pits for fuel and a rear tyre change, Chassagne took over the lead. 'Very gradually Chassagne increased his advantage over four laps, to the enthusiasm of the French spectators, who were delighted at a French car and a French driver getting ahead, cheering him constantly as he flashed past the stand.' For six laps in all the Frenchman held off the entire Duesenberg team. Then came disaster for the Ballot. It may have been a stone tearing away a bracket, or a fracture from a severe jolt. Suddenly the fuel tank dropped on to the propeller shaft, which tore a hole in it. Chassagne limped into the pit with petrol flowing out — and was hustled into the dead car park.

By the twentieth lap it was Duesenberg — Duesenberg — Ballot — Ballot — and the road surface was breaking up at every corner, adding lap by lap to the density of flying stones. Guyot's mechanic was struck on the head, and had to be replaced, Lee Guinness was bleeding, and Segrave's mechanic was also knocked out. Joe Boyer took over the lead when Chassagne retired, had his radiator pierced by a stone, and lost so much water that a big-end seized up. His car was stranded at Tertre Rouge, and Murphy took over the lead, closely followed by Guyot in the third Duesenberg. DePalma pressed relentlessly, and Goux in the 2 litre Ballot was coming up well in support. The pace was beginning to tell on the American cars. Guyot's Duesenberg was suffering from clutch slip, and after stopping out on the circuit he brought it hesitantly to the pits. His mechanic was too tired and injured about the face to crank the car into life again. Last minute drama was provided by the ace driver Duray, who had been watching the race and, realizing Guyot's predicament, leapt the fence and 'in white cuffs and black clothes, took the place of the worn out mechanic.'

This was a blow to the American team, for the Duesenberg fell back to sixth place as a result of the delay. And seconds later it was seen that the leader

1923

81. *European Grand Prix, Monza. Salamano with his Type 805 supercharged Fiat, the victory smile already on his face*

82. *The tank exposed. Ultra short-wheelbase, ultra unmanageable Bugatti (enveloping bodywork here missing) for the 1923 French Grand Prix*

1924

83. *And a year later, the classical shape has arrived. Type 35 Bugatti in the 1924 French Grand Prix*

82

was in trouble, too. Murphy had been driving magnificently, lapping with splendid consistency, never allowing himself to be rattled by the performance of the more ebullient French drivers on the corners. He had a lead of fifteen minutes over his fellow-countryman DePalma in the first of the Ballots. He was some twenty miles from the flag when a large stone struck his radiator and another broke his thermometer. Murphy had already seen his team-mate Boyer fall out of the race from the same cause. With one lap to go he came into his pit, changed his rear tyres, which were almost down to the canvas, looked anxiously at his leaking radiator without switching off, decided

that it was useless to take off the cap as he would not be able to top up with cold water, and drove away carefully.

It said much for the Duesenberg brothers' engine that it covered not only another $10\frac{1}{2}$ miles but completed another full lap in error with an empty radiator, crossing the line again just ahead of DePalma in the first Ballot.

It was a magnificent win, which surprised the French, and greatly raised the prestige of American racing cars in Europe. American Indianapolis cars were to cross the Atlantic again in pursuit of Grand Prix prizes; but never again were they even to come close to success.

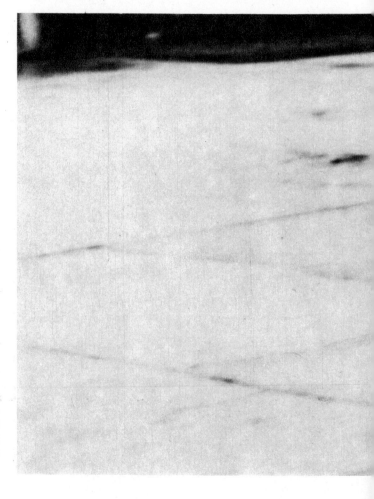

87. And as a contrast with some of the riches from Molsheim, here is one of the shortest-lived racing cars of all time — the remarkable 806 Fiat, a 12-cylinder supercharged car which walked away with the Milan Grand Prix in 1927, and was ne'er seen again

Jimmy Murphy and his white Duesenberg stand alone in the Grand Prix records as a magnificent tribute to a great driver and one of the finest racing car designs of all time.

1926

84. Le Patron, *Ettore Bugatti* left, with his driver Jules Goux and Senor Rezola at San Sebastian after winning the European Grand Prix

1927

85. Mme Elisabeth Junek during the practice period for the 1927 Targa Florio with her 2 litre Bugatti

86. Type 35 Bugatti at La Garoupe Grand Prix, 1927. The driver is Philippe Entancelin

Italy and Britain Invade the United States

An American Duesenberg wins the French Grand Prix! An Italian Maserati wins the Indianapolis 500! Eighteen years separated these two sensational motor racing occasions which upset the established order and brought fame to the victorious.

European domination of the American classic was ended in 1920 by an American Monroe, powered by an engine based in principle on Henri's Peugeot and designed by a brilliant young engineer, Cornelius W. Van Ranst. Neither the European designers — nor the Duesenbergs for that matter — could match Van Ranst's 8-cylinder machine the following year. Another young engineer, Harry Miller, entered the Indianapolis scene in 1922 with a 32-valve straight-eight unit having much in common with the Duesenberg engine. In spite of his successes with Duesenbergs, Jimmy Murphy preferred the Miller engine, transplanted it to his Duesenberg chassis — and proved the success of his hybrid by winning, with two laps to spare.

Throughout the 1920's and 1930's Indianapolis track racing, like European Grand Prix racing, became more and more dominated by the home side. Ballots, old Peugeots, a full team of Mercedes, a mammoth V16 Maserati, among many others, wrestled with the Americans round the brickyard. None gained any significant honours. The reason was not hard to find. Indianapolis racing was becoming more and more specialized as a result of the concentrated application of engineers of the calibre of Harry Miller and the Duesenbergs on the problem of how to travel faster round a geometric oval. In Europe racing car designers had to build (as they do today) cars for 20 m.p.h. hairpins, flat-out turns, steep gradients as well as long straights.

In the 1920's Miller-engined and Duesenberg-engined cars duelled annually at Indy, first one, then the other, gaining the upper hand. Tuned induction systems on the Millers were matched by the introduction of superchargers by the Duesenbergs. Influenced by the first ever 100 m.p.h. lap by an ancient front-drive

Early Indianapolis

1919
88. Duesenberg's first effort was a failure

1921
89. Three great Indy figures: Tommy Milton, Barney Oldfield, Louis Chevrolet

1922
90. Jimmy Murphy, this year's winner

1923
91. Three minutes to go

1934
92. Bill Cummings, victor at 104.863 m.p.h.

1936
93. Rex Mays in a Miller-powered Gilmore Special

1931

94. Wilbur Shaw, first man to win three times at Indy, still had some lessons to learn in 1931. How to avoid going over the wall was one of them

Christie (it was a 20 litre car when the regulations permitted nothing over 2014 c.c., so it wasn't allowed to race!) Jimmy Murphy ordered a front-drive racer from Harry Miller in 1923. Murphy was killed before he could use it, but the new Miller — the '91' — was a sensation. Intercoolers to chill the supercharged mixture were used by Frank Lockhart in his Miller, the winner in 1926. The Duesenbergs gave their undivided genius to the chassis, and came up with an offset frame with engine and shaft angled to allow a lower profile, and axles offset to meet the peculiar centrifugal demands of the left-hand curves. In 1933, when the capacity limit was already up to 6 litres, Miller and his chief engineer produced a 4.2 litre twin-cam, sixteen-valve 'four' based on one of the company's marine engines with which they had already had racing experience. This formed the basis for the longest-lived and most successful racing engine in Indianapolis history: the Offenhauser, after Fred Offenhauser to whom Miller sold out in 1934.

The 'Offy' had already achieved domination by 1938, when Floyd Roberts won at a record 117.2 m.p.h. But history was made again the following year by a driver whom many think the greatest ever in Indy annals. Wilbur Shaw had already won in 1937 in an Offy-engined car, driving without a single stop for fuel, and he placed second in 1938. But Shaw had

his shrewd eyes on European cars. By 1937 a new generation of vast and tremendously powerful cars had brought about a renaissance to a dying sport across the Atlantic. Some of these machines had demonstrated their speed and roadholding at the revived Vanderbilt Cup on the Roosevelt Raceway in July 1937. Here the Millers were utterly routed. 'There is no question,' one eyewitness reported, 'but that the American public were astounded at the extraordinary speed of the cars . . . Nothing quite like these machines has ever been seen before in the States, nor had anyone really believed in their reputation beforehand.'

Shaw himself was there, and was properly astounded, too. He persuaded his sponsor, Mike Boyle, to buy an Italian Maserati for the next Indianapolis 500. Unfortunately, due to language difficulties, the Italian company sent a supercharged $1\frac{1}{2}$ litre instead of the 8CTF 3 litre Shaw had set his eyes on. The next year Boyle's chief mechanic was sent to Italy. The bigger Maserati was just what was needed. The independent front suspension, when properly set up for Indy's turns, allowed Shaw to go through them faster than his rivals, and the supercharged straight-eight out-powered the 4-cylinder Offy. Shaw went on to win — and repeated his triumph a year later, the first man ever to win twice successively.

The arrival of the European Grand Prix Maserati

The Winners

95. **1905** *Young Frank Lockhart's Miller*

96. **1946** *George Robson, with nine-year-old Thorne Engineering Special*

97. **1947** *Mauri Rose, who won in 1948 also*

98. **1949** *Bill Holland, who put the speed over the 120- mark*

99. **1950** *Johnnie Parsons, winner in the rain*

100. **1951** *Lee Wallard, 'small engine' winner*

101. **1952** Troy Ruttman — 128.922 m.p.h.

102. **1954** Bill Vukovitch — winner 1953 and 1954

103. **1955** Bob Sweikert — 128.209 m.p.h. — slowest since '51

104. **1956** Pat Flaherty — John Zink Special

105. **1957** Sam Hanks — topped the 135 m.p.h. mark

caused a sensation at Indianapolis. Other drivers went shopping in Europe, and European drivers crossed the Atlantic with their cars. The effect was like a shot in the arm for American racing. Here was the evidence that science, applied to engine, suspension and aerodynamics could bring about greater speed as well as greater reliability. A new era of refreshing technical enterprise set in at Indianapolis, and for the next decade some fascinating and ingenious machines were seen at the brickyard.

Among those who were galvanized into exciting experimentation was Harry Miller — sold out but not played out. He made an extraordinary come-back with the Miller-Gulf Special — which had the engine at the rear like the German Auto-Union, and disc brakes — a specification that we may well see repeated during the life of the current 3 litre formula, more than a quarter century later. There's a prophetic mind for you! Miller's ex-chief engineer, Leo Goosen, came up with a remarkably advanced V8 engine in 1941, with four gear-driven overhead camshafts and a centrifugal supercharger. The Novi engine was to have a long history at Indy right up to 1965, always supported by faith, never by success.

Eccentricity reached a climax in the late 1940's. There was the Pat Clancy Special, with six wheels for adhesion, in 1948; and two years earlier the Twin

106

106.   **1958** *Jimmy Bryan — 133.791 m.p.h.*

107.   **1962** *Rodger Ward — the roadster in its ultimate form*

108.   **1963** *Parnelli Jones — a controversial victory*

109.   **1964** *A. J. Foyt — last win for the big roadster*

110.   **1965** *Jim Clark makes it at last*

107

108

109

110

Coach, a truly bizarre construction featuring a blown $1\frac{1}{2}$ litre Miller engine at front and rear, the driver sitting amidships on top of the superchargers. It might have had a great future, having qualified for the front row, but got 'hung on the wall' after a few laps — which in Indy jargon means crashed against the barrier, usually due to excessive driving zeal. Even supercharged diesel truck engines were tried, and went very fast. While the Novis continued to travel very fast, holding the four-lap qualifying record from 1946 to 1951, Frank Kurtis's tubular-framed cars showed up better in the record books with a successive first, second and third.

So far all this activity at Indianapolis was lively and interesting; but, while the brickyard can never by any stretch become a dull place, and the winning speed rose from 119.81 m.p.h. in 1948 to 133.79 m.p.h. ten years, later, technical sterility began to set in during the 1950's and early 1960's. This was the era of the massive roadsters, technically refined to the ultimate point but mainly non-innovatory; and the final era of the magnificent 4-cylinder Offenhauser engine, finally reduced in weight by fifty pounds, and putting out 450 h.p. from under 4.2 litres.

The early 1960's at Indianapolis, then, like the late 1930's, was a period that seemed ripe for a foreign invasion, in spite of the abortive efforts by Ferrari

and Maserati to break through in 1952, 1956 and
1959. In Europe a new scientific revolution was under
way, featuring simplicity, lightness, new standards
of balance and adhesion, and reduced frontal area.
The pioneers were the Coopers, father and son, who
worked from a little garage at Surbiton in the London
suburbs. They had already recorded astonishing successes, notably in the smaller Formula II and Formula
III fields, when they decided to throw their meagre
resources and considerable genius into Formula I
Grand Prix racing. Driving the rear-engined Cooper,
Stirling Moss astonished the Establishment by winning
the Argentine Grand Prix with an under-engined
car in 1958, and Jack Brabham took the World Championship in 1959 and 1960 in a developed and enlarged
version of the same car.

In 1961 Jack Brabham brought one of these 'pint-
sized' racers to Indianapolis. Among the giant roadsters
it looked like a toy — no one could qualify *that* at the
brickyard! Good for a laugh, old boy, but . . .! Then
the railbirds began to watch the laughable little Cooper
on the turns. It was going fast round them — it wasn't
even slowing for them. No one had ever seen anything
like it. Of course, with an engine nearly $1\frac{1}{2}$ litres smaller
than the Offy it couldn't match the roadsters on the
straights. But the sensation of the qualifying period
was the Australian's place on the fifth row.

The Cooper went through the 500 without any
troubles — except excessive tyre wear, which caused
Brabham to limit himself to 140 m.p.h. laps. And he
sailed effortlessly and impressively into ninth place.

Brabham was inexperienced at Indianapolis. His
pit stops were awful, sometimes taking over a minute.
He was under-engined. And the tyres weren't right.
But in balance and roadholding the little Cooper
was far ahead of the American roadsters. Th tubular
frame weighed almost nothing. The Climax engine
weighed 290 pounds against 490 for the Offenhauser.

Here was food for thought, you would imagine.
And what happened? Practically everyone at Indianapolis went on just as if the established order of things
could never change, as if the massive roadsters and
the 490-pound Offy would go on forever. And a glance
at the record books shows that the die-hard conser-
vatives were half-right after all, for front-engined,
rear-driven, Offy-powered roadsters won again for
the next three years.

Only one American showed himself ready to accept
the new technical advances learned in Europe and
demonstrated at Indianapolis. He was Mickey Thompson, a top hot-rod man, who perusaded the Harvey
Aluminium Company –– for whom he acted as automobile consultant — to sign up John Crosthwaite,
formerly of Coopers, to design a car for 1962. The

56

Engines and Bodies

1941
111. Indy's own Auto-Union: four-wheel-drive, rear engine, and loads of trouble. The enterprising Miller-Gulf Special

1915
112. The diesel promised well, but never quite made it. This is Jimmy Jackson's Cummins which went out with a broken vibration damper after 130 miles

1954
113. The fierce and handsome V8 Novis will go down in Indy legend as one of the great lost causes

1955
114. Jimmy Daywalt's car in 1955 was fully faired and fendered, but had to be stripped down

1957
115. Sam Hanks' Belond Exhaust Special, with the 4-cylinder Offenhauser, tilted 18 degrees.

115

machine had much in common with the Cooper, with tubular space-frame 'chassis', independent suspension front and rear by wishbones — and behind the driver one of the new very light Buick V8 stock engines, enlarged from 3.5 to 4.2 litres. Dan Gurney, who had already won his laurels in Europe, drove the car and qualified it at a surprising 147.9 m.p.h. — and showed that he could go through the turns at a fantastic 146 m.p.h. But Gurney dropped out early in the race after holding the big roadsters ... and the rear-engined scientists had failed again.

In 1963 the European-inspired assault was renewed on a larger scale, the Thompson cars being joined by a name new to Indy, Lotus. Like the Cooper, Lotus racing sports cars and Grand Prix cars, products of the fertile brain of the young engineer Colin Chapman, had already scored numerous successes in Britain and on the Continent. His first whippy little Grand Prix machines had been front-engined rear-driven cars, but after Cooper had shown the way, Chapman had switched to the rear-engined layout. The tiny space-frame Lotus 24 with Coventry-Climax V8 engine gave huge promise; the Lotus 25 set new chassis standards with a remarkable light alloy 'monocoque' stretched-skin main structure, combining great strength with very low weight. Scottish driver Jim Clark took it to its first victory in the Belgian Grand Prix in June 1962. By then Colin Chapman already had his sights on the richest and most famous race in America. He now determined to make a real showing there in 1963, using his monocoque ultra-lightweight car. But he needed a bigger engine than any British manufacturer could provide. Where should he go for his power?

At this time the giant American Ford company was showing a renewed interest in competition work, and when approached by Chapman the chiefs at Dearborn said they thought that they could help. The unit chosen was the stock Fairlane V8. After experiments with twin-cam, four-valves-per-cylinder heads, they decided to revert to pushrod-operated valves; and it was this unit, with Italian Colotti gearbox, that Chapman married to his modified Lotus 25 structure, now redesignated the Lotus 29. Two Lotus-Fords came to the brickyard in 1963. This time the British cars were not treated in the light-hearted manner of two years earlier.

The Thompson cars made a poor showing, but Chapman's shrewd scientific approach to race tactics began to emerge when he held his cars back early on, relying on the time he would save with a single pit stop against the three stops of the favourite roadsters; and Parnelli Jones's A. J. Watson-prepared Arganjanian-Willard was the hottest favourite. This way Clark saved some forty seconds — but gained no benefit because Parnelli Jones's halts were made while the yellow lights were on, forbidding passing

1961

116. 117. *The new shape at Indy. Here is Brabham's Climax-engined Cooper, too underpowered for the American roadsters, though its speed through the turns caused some hard thinking*

1964

118. *Everything has been tried once at Indy, though Bobby Jones' Offy-engined side-car crashed in practice*

119. *Mickey Thompson followed the Cooper lead, and his cars brought new American hopes and a new frontal aspect to the brickyard. It was a brave and expensive effort that never quite paid off*

The Brickyard's Hazards

1949

120. Bill Holland tears through the flames left by the 'Voodoo V8' Novi — and on to victory

1952

121. The Italian invasion in the early 1950's never got off the ground, in spite of Ferrari omnipotence in Europe. World Champion Alberto Ascari was the only one to qualify, and here he makes a dramatic exit when the spokes of his left rear wheel yield under the strain imposed by Indy's curves

and limiting speed. Clark and the Lotus-Ford had to be content with a second.

After this performance, it was clear to all but dyed-in-the-wool traditionalists that the shape and form of the Indy cars must change. And yet the day of the roadster was not yet done. Lotus came back on the offensive again in 1964, now a dangerous, and feared, enemy. The extent of their influence was clear to every one of the 325,000 spectators at the track: for of the thirty-three qualifiers on the grid no less than twelve were rear-engined, five of them with Offy engines behind the driver, and seven with the V8 Ford unit, now much more modified. Furthermore, at the end of the first lap the first three — two Lotuses and Rodger Ward's Kaiser Aluminium Special — were all rear-engined. Tragedy struck minutes later, two American drivers dying in an inferno of blazing fuel, and the race was halted for an hour and forty-five minutes. When the fight was resumed, four of the 'new generation' machines took the first places. At the forty-seventh lap Scottish driver, English car, American engine, were comfortably in the lead. The foreign invasion seemed to have succeeded at last — no one looked like getting near to Clark's Lotus — until his tyre treads began peeling off!

Motor racing is an unpredictable business. Who could believe that, with all the experience of high speed driving on air-filled rubber over some seventy years, this sort of thing could happen at less than quarter distance at Indianapolis? But tyre failure settled the 1964 500, as it had decided the pattern of many an earlier brickyard duel. Loss of tyre tread upset the delicately balanced rear suspension, which collapsed under the strain; and the flying Scotsman drew into the pits amid a cloud of sparks, one rear wheel flat on the ground! A. J. Foyt, winner in 1961 when the first of the British rear-engined cars set the crowds chuckling, sailed home a comfortable winner in one of the last of the handsome, mighty front-engined roadsters. Perhaps it was the last ever victory for what the older generation still regard as a 'proper racing car'.

The total rout of the great Indy roadsters was completed in 1965. Few of the drivers would have anything to do with them. 1963 winner Parnelli Jones and 1964 winner A. J. Foyt were both in re-worked 1964 Lotus-Fords — and the wonderful old Offy was almost out of the picture, although one front-engined roadster managed sixth place.

Clark's triumph was one of the most epochal in motor racing history, certainly in British annals. He was the first British driver ever to win at the brickyard, since the race began in 1911. And his winning speed was the first ever over the 150 m.p.h. figure, which few

1961

122. *Rear-engine, four wheel independent suspension, disc brakes, four-speed gearbox, 550 pounds less weight — these were the advantages that sent Brabham faster through the curves — although he could summon only some 250 horses against the roadsters' 400*

1964

123. *By the following year, rear-engine advocates were growing in numbers. Here Jim Clark's Lotus heads the pack. But this was before tyre troubles intervened*

prophets even five years before had thought attainable. He won by the driving skill of a real world champion, in the fastest, most scientifically designed, most shrewdly prepared car, rigidly controlled by the best tactical and strategical team in the business. Colin Chapman met the demands of the new rule requiring two pit stops and a maximum fuel capacity of 75 gallons (imposed as a result of the awful fire in 1964) by running on gasoline-based fuel instead of the methanol used by his closest rivals. Petrol in the Ford-engined Lotus cut top speed by perhaps 3 m.p.h.; but this loss was more than made up by lower consumption, and the need for only the two required pit stops instead of the three demanded by the less economical methanol-burners.

Jim Clark was well in the lead when he pitted on his sixty-sixth lap. Second man Foyt took command, then yielded first place to Clark again when he came in. And at half-way (100 laps) it was Clark, Foyt, Parnelli Jones — the Scotsman lapping at an incredible 155 m.p.h. When the Lotus was called in thirty-six laps later it had such a lead that it was away again without losing it — and that had rarely been seen in recent years at Indy. Clark was running with the computer-like regularity the European crowds had seen so often. It didn't seem possible that he could make an error of judgement — and the Ford engine was as crisp

1963

124. Dwarf among the giants. Lotus bunched among the roadsters aptly demonstrates the rear-engine revolution

1965

125. The great Parnelli Jones at last bows to the inevitable. Strip off the advertising and this might be Clark at Silverstone

The Agony of the Race

1952
126. Ruttman pits — a frenetic pause in his hot duel with Vukovitch

1954
127. A drama lost to European racing for so long!
130. They say it's the worst ordeal of all!

1963
128. The heat of the chase. Jim Clark positions himself to pass Don Branson
129. Pitting — with all the refinements! And they helped Parnelli Jones to his tight 1963 victory

as when it had started. By one hundred and fifty laps Clark could afford to ease off — and let the others catch up a few seconds. And that gesture appeared as the final — and almost insulting — confirmation that the old regime was over, a new sovereign had triumphed at the historic Indiana battlefield — the Indy brickyard.

1964

131. *V8 Novi makes a fast pit stop*

1965

132. *Lotus and Jim Clark make it at last, at the third try*

15

1938

Plate 15. Mercedes team manager Alfred Neubauer surveys the circuit with a conqueror's eye. French Grand Prix, Rheims, 1938. His cars came in 1—2—3. Detachable wheel facilitates cockpit entry and exit

Plate 16. By the late 1930's Bugatti could no longer hold the German cars on the Grand Prix circuits. But was there ever a lovelier racing car than the 3.3, here hill-climbing in the hands of J. Lemon Burton?

16

1939

Plates 17. 18. History repeated. Weeks before the military invasion in 1914 the Germans came to France for the Grand Prix and proved victorious. In 1939 they came back again. This time Mercedes failed after leading, but Auto-Unions took the first two places at Rheims. The French had only outclassed Talbots and Delahayes with which to fight back, but took third and fourth. Above: Etancelin's Talbot Right: the winning Auto-Union of Muller, his first Grand Prix victory. The V12 machine averaged 105.24 m.p.h.

17

1939

Plate 19.   Brooklands, home of British motor racing from 1907, had its last season in 1939. This is Kenneth Evans's Alfa Romeo, shortly before the war closed the circuit for ever

19

A Golden Era (1934-1939)

133. Louis Chiron, one of the few survivors from Grand Prix racing's golden age in the 1930's, demonstrates the contemporary driving style — close against the wheel, arms crossed

1931

134. Franco-Italian duel before the German onslaught. 1931 Belgian Grand Prix. Nuvolari is in number 10 'Monza' Scuderia Ferrari Alfa Romeo; Williams's Bugatti number 4 was the winner

In February 1934 news of two Grand Prix projects began to trickle out of Germany, a nation which had taken little interest in motor racing since the triumphant racing car invasion of France in 1914. This certainly caused a flutter of interest, for when Germany goes motor racing, she takes the business seriously. But the first announcements were modest enough — a photograph of an odd-looking beast called an Auto-Union (a name new to motor racing), and a drawing of 'the new single-seater racing Mercedes' (a name old and distinguished in motor racing). Few people could be expected to recognize the significance of this news, or understand that a new age of motor racing was about to open up, an age that was to be one of the most glorious in racing history.

This is what had happened. In 1933 Adolf Hitler, of infamous memory, came into power in Germany. Among the many decisions he reached was that Germany should return to motor racing — return and win, and not only win but utterly annihilate the opposition. Hitler knew quite a lot about racing cars, and he wisely recognized the prestige benefits to science and industry that Germany would derive from success in the Grand Prix field. And not only prestige. His intention was to encourage German design teams to develop new engines, new metals, new methods of construction that could later be used in the fleets of fighting aircraft, swift torpedo boats and tanks that he was also planning for the glory of the Greater Reich. In hard cash for a start he offered a prize of £40,000 to the constructor of the most successful German racing car in 1934. What was added to this under the counter will never be known.

Two German design teams set off after that prize. One was led by Hans Nibel and Max Wagner of Daimler-Benz at Stuttgart (the two companies had combined forces and names some six years earlier). The other was led by Ferdinand Porsche, whose lifetime of brilliant work was to extend from the Prince Henry Trial Austrian-Daimler of 1910, to Volkswagen, Tiger tank and the car that bears his name today. The name

1935

135. Straight-eight Alfa Romeo, showing the more enveloping bodywork to combat the Germans. For this year the engine was enlarged to 3.2 litres, and front independent springing was tried

1937

136. Alfa Romeo was still struggling to regain ascendancy. Now they had a V12 4 litre engine, and independent suspension all round

137. More and more the Italian Alfa Romeos were obliged to conform with the German profile, although they could no longer match either chassis or engines of Mercedes-Benz and Auto-Union

of the car that he and his team were to create in 1934, the Auto-Union, derived from the 'union' of four small manufacturers, including Horch and D.K.W. Governed only by a weight restriction of 750 kg. and a minimum body width of 33½ inches — the new 1934 formula — these teams came up with two fascinating but quite different interpretations on the same theme.

Early in 1934 the cars were tested, semi-publicly, at Monza in Italy. And slowly, week by week, the formidable nature of this new German threat to the established constructors of racing cars — Alfa Romeo, Maserati and Bugatti — came to be recognized.

Of the two German cars the Auto-Union was the more menacing and more unusual in appearance, although there were natural suspicions of its eccentricity. Ferdinand Porsche had decided to put the engine behind the driver — and what an engine! A V16 of no less than 4.36 litres, with two valves per cylinder all operated by a single overhead camshaft — the inlet valves directly, the exhaust valves through pushrods and rockers. Assisted by a Roots-type blower, the output was 295 h.p. at a modest 4,500 r.p.m. Working forward from the engine there were situated, in this order, the fuel tank, driver and radiator; the whole being supported within a tubular framework consisting of two parallel side members united by cross members. Suspension was independent to all four wheels, those at the front each being supported by two trailing arms, the lower of which was coupled to a torsion bar; the rear geometry following the less radical swing axle layout. The result was a hideous monstrosity, the ugliest thing on four wheels ever seen on a race track, but also one of the most formidable, with a tremendously high power-to-weight ratio. Some people — especially the drivers — wondered how it would handle.

The Mercedes-Benz was less unorthodox, but quite as epochal. Its 3.36 straight-eight engine, at the front and driving the rear wheels, put out some 350 h.p. on its first tests, against the 200 or so h.p. of the contemporary Italian racing engines. It was housed in a sheet steel box section frame that was both rigid and very light, and like the rival Auto-Union all four wheels were independently suspended. Both cars were clothed in a light alloy body, and their low sleek appearance, with the driver nestled down in a faired cockpit, was in marked contrast with the upright unaerodynamic aspect of the French and Italian Grand Prix contemporaries.

The established designs against which the German cars were to range themselves during the 1934 racing season were the P3, or B2600, Alfa Romeo, the 8-cylinder twin-supercharged 2.65 litre brainchild of Vittorio Jano; the Maserati brothers' 2.9 litre straight-eight; and the Type 59 Bugatti, Ettore's latest creation from his works at Molsheim, a twin-cam supercharged

138. *Grotesque, unmanageable and exceedingly ingenious —*
Auto-Union

139. *By 1937 the Mercedes-Benz formelrennwagen W125*
was up to 5.66 litres, and was turning out almost 650 b.h.p.

140. *Hans Stuck was one of the few drivers to master the*
Auto-Union

141. 142. 143. *The 1937 Berlin Avus-Rennen revealed the new silver projectiles at their most spectacular. Above: the start Below: fully enveloped Mercedes-Benz and Auto-Union on the banking. Hermann Lang's average was as fast as today's Indianapolis speeds — 162.62 m.p.h.*

144. *W125 1937 Mercedes-Benz: 'the office'*

and exquisitely beautiful machine.

The 1934 Grand Prix season opened in an atmosphere heavy with expectation and anxiety, although for a time it seemed as if the assault from the new German forces would fail and the established order would prevail once again. The German cars were, after all, entirely new, in many ways experimental. They were up against drivers of the calibre of Nuvolari, Varzi, Chiron, Campari — long experienced with their cars and with the tricky racing circuits of Europe.

Neither of the German teams turned up at Monte Carlo for the Monaco Grand Prix. At the Avus track in the Berlin suburbs a few weeks later, where the Germans ran a short race outside the Formula, Mercedes withdrew their entries at the last minute, and the Auto-Unions were utterly routed — though very fast. At another short event on the winding, mountainous Nurburgring the 'silver torpedoes' appeared together in strength — and the finishing order was Mercedes followed by Auto-Union. But the Alfa team of Enzo Ferrari (later to become the most famous racing car constructor of all time) was not fully represented. And the first real clash was postponed until the French Grand Prix. Memories went back to an earlier German invasion, just twenty years before, when Peugeot had fought bitterly and for long against Mercedes at this same event. The signs were as ominous

145. *Mercedes-Benz pit stops, under the command of the fierce Alfred Neubauer (in trilby) were swift and spectacular*

146. *Bernd Rosemeyer, greatest of all the Auto-Union drivers, talks over an imminent record-breaking attempt with Ferdinand Porsche, the machine's designer*

147. *Von Delius's expression reveals the responsibilities of putting an Auto-Union through a corner*

148. *The W125 Mercedes-Benz was much more tractable, if still requiring skill and strength unknown to present-day Grand Prix drivers*

147

148

for the blue Bugattis and red Alfas in 1934 as they had been for the Peugeots of 1914.

The 1934 French Grand Prix was held on the combined winding road circuit and steeply banked autodrome at Montlhéry. From the very beginning it was a battle royal, one of the most exciting and desperate races ever seen in Europe. Thirteen cars appeared on the burning hot afternoon of July 1st, lined up on the narrow concrete strip between the packed stands ranging up high on both sides. All the great teams of the day were represented, the two silver Auto-Unions and three silver Mercedes appearing like pencil-thin projectiles beside the tall, stark French and Italian machines.

Practice times had revealed the Germans as fast, very fast — but no faster than the most determined Italian and French drivers. In the front rank were Hans Stuck's Auto-Union and Varzi with the fastest of the Scuderia Ferrari Alfa Romeos. German cars alone occupied the second row, Momberger's Auto-Union and the first Mercedes driver, Rudolf Caracciola. Behind them were ranged Chiron with the second of the Alfas and Benoist's and Nuvolari's Bugattis; then Count Trossi (Alfa Romeo) and Dreyfus (Bugatti); Etancelin and Zehender (Maseratis) and von Brauchitsch in the second Mercedes; and taking up the rear, the third Mercedes, in the hands of Fagioli. It was the most interesting Grand Prix line-up since 1923.

This is how Barré Lyndon saw the start, as he related in his magnificent book, *Grand Prix*:

Not until barely sixty seconds remained were the engines started up ... Exhaust notes roared out, rising swiftly to a blast of tremendous sound which echoed across the great track and reached the crowds lining the *circuit routier,* beyond the narrow exit towards which the machines faced. Mechanics ran from the cars as the starter poised his flag and, during the moments before the flag dropped, Chiron's Alfa-Romeo began to roll forward as if its driver was impatient and eager to get away. Suddenly the flag fell and, at that, Chiron's scarlet machine hurled itself away from the line in one magnificent burst of acceleration.

The car shot past Caracciola's Mercedes before the German driver had moved a yard, then raced by Stuck, snatching the lead almost before the folds of the flag had brushed the concrete.

The Frenchman was at the height of his powers, and utterly determined to hold off the German threat. He left the autodrome like a bullet, on to the long winding road circuit, a good three lengths ahead of Caracciola's Mercedes. The screaming bunch faded from view, lost in distant combat among the woods and meadows to the south. Five minutes later — an incredibly short time — the scream of superchargers

and howl of exhausts was heard again, rapidly increasing in intensity as the pack raced towards the east side of the autodrome. A wave of agonized expectation rippled through the crowds. Who would it be? There was a blur of red — someone shouted 'Chiron!' And there was the Alfa, high on the banking. But not alone. Hard behind flashed a silver machine — who was it? Impossible to tell at this speed. Then, 'Caracciola!'

Behind was another Mercedes, just ahead of a third silver car, later seen to be the fastest Auto-Union, Hans Stuck's. Varzi's Alfa held grimly on behind the Germans, in support of the flying Chiron who was holding off the van of the Teutonic attack.

There was much passing and re-passing on the road circuit on the next laps, and when the tight leading bunch reappeared — average speed was up now towards 90 m.p.h. — Stuck had thrust his Auto-Union past both Mercedes, and had the stubby nose of his machine almost against Chiron's rear wheels. Round the banking they soared, a magnificent blend of blue, scarlet and silver, and dived down once again between the stands. It seemed impossible that Chiron could hold off the German challenge any longer — and minutes later far away at Les Biscornes corner, the Auto-Union at last forced its way through, leaving a trail of gravel and black rubber on the road.

Back on the autodrome Stuck's lead was five seconds, and the crowd rose together in dismay and urged on their hero. Chiron needed no encouragement. He knew that the honour of France rested on his shoulders, for the blue Bugattis were fast failing and showed no speed. But he was a shrewd fighter. It was a long race, and there was time enough to regain the lead. All he had to do for the present was to keep the Auto-Union in sight and in striking distance. This he did with prodigious skill and nerve, sometimes coming up close to rattle the German, then slipping back a few lengths. No matter what Stuck did — and he raised the lap speed higher and higher towards 90 m.p.h. — he could not throw off the Frenchman in the 'old fashioned' Italian car.

At the ninth lap it was Auto-Union, Alfa Romeo, Mercedes, Mercedes — then a gap to Varzi in the next Alfa fighting it out with the third Mercedes. The leading Mercedes were ordered to put on the pressure for fear they would lose touch with Stuck and Chiron. Chiron answered by putting his foot hard down again, testing Stuck's nerves to the utmost. The gap between silver and red was down to four lengths on the banking — and on one of the short straights of the road section the stark red Alfa thundered by. Again the crowd rose, this time to cheer.

Far back in the field the first signs of a crack in the

1937

149. When the German racing cars first came to Britain, they were a revelation in speed and spectacle. Auto-Union, at Donington Park, cornering

150. The same car airborne

151. 1938 Auto-Union, a new design by Fuereisen and von Eberhorst with 90 degree V12 engine — still, of course, at the rear

German assault showed when Momberger retired his Auto-Union. The pace was too much for the Germans. Stuck came in to change worn tyres — lost two minutes, and now it was up to the Mercedes to chase Chiron. There followed another tremendous duel, led by Fagioli — an Italian in a German car versus a Frenchman in an Italian car, each striving to break the nerve, or the engine, of the other. The lap speed went up to over 90 m.p.h., and the rest of the field — even Caracciola — fell behind!

Of course it could not last. Chiron broke the record, and the Mercedes's attack, on the same lap. Fagioli fell behind, stopped at the roadside, and climbed out. Chiron had won again. He had defeated in fair fight the new Auto-Union and the new Mercedes — from which so much had been expected — in turn. And he was now so far ahead that he could afford to relax for a while.

The pace set by Louis Chiron's Alfa Romeo had not only broken his direct challengers. Far behind him the other Germans met trouble one by one as a result of the strain they had put on their new cars. Stuck regained ground and challenged the Alfas again, but the strength had gone out of his punch, and he was now demoralized by the failure of his fellowcountrymen. His car was losing water at an alarming rate, from leaks caused by vibration in the frame tubes through which the radiator water was passed to the

1938

152. 153. The new Grand Prix cars of the 1930's called for a new breed of driver who could cope with the vastly increased power — note wheelspin on acceleration at right — and above: muscular demands. This is Rudolf Caracciola, with Nuvolari, Rosemeyer and von Stuck among the greatest of this age. 'Carach' was an experienced driver by 1934, but the new Mercedes cars provided him with the opportunity to show his wonderful prowess

engine. He came in once again, did a lap, retired.

It was as if the last of the enemy had fled the field of battle. The leading Alfas began to play among themselves to celebrate. The young Guy Moll had taken over Trossi's car, and he went after Varzi. Second and third places changed more than once — until the flag fell at last, and the three red Scuderia Ferrari machines crossed the line.

Instead of being annihilated by Hitler's new racing machines, the P3 Alfas had utterly routed every one of them. But the French Grand Prix of 1934 was the last major race in Europe to be dominated by the handsome old-style racing car, with non-independent suspension, large frontal area, and high seating. The song of the Alfas at Montlhéry was magnificent to the ear — but it was a swan song nevertheless. Science and money must win — and most people knew it. Germany had too much at stake to afford a repeat of this humiliation.

Back at Chemnitz — home of Auto-Union — and at Stuttgart, the postmortems were soon in full swing. Facts and figures were urgently analyzed, drivers interrogated, stresses re-calculated, and reliability as well as power sought after.

The new pattern, the new order, was set at the Nurburgring two weeks later, when the best that Chiron could do was to get within six minutes of Fagioli's Mercedes, itself two minutes behind Stuck's Auto-Union at the end. After this it was only rarely that either Alfa Romeo or Maserati were able to hold the fast and now highly efficient German cars. The Italian engineers sought, and acquired, more power for their machines. Engine sizes were increased again and again, body contours were smoothed, independent suspension was incorporated, and every sort of ingenuity was exercised. But with all the skill in the world, these were only makeshift expedients, and the results could not match the power, speed, braking, suspension and balance of the German machines, conceived as a whole and supported with almost limitless funds.

Between 1934 and 1937 the Mercedes-Benz engine grew to 5.66 litres, and in this form produced close to 650 h.p. The Auto-Union went up to over 6 litres, but it was not as reliable as the Stuttgart car, and it was difficult to find anyone to drive it, such was the unpredictability of its cornering. The tide of German success was unbroken by the introduction of a new formula, limiting engine size to 3 litres, for 1938. Both Auto-Union and Daimler-Benz remained loyal to their rear- and front-engined layouts, and both chose V12's for their new source of power, although there were fundamental differences between the two. Gamely, Alfa Romeo struggled back into the ring either with 8-, 12-, or 16-cylinder engines in all-independent chassis based on their earlier attempt

153

155. Omnipotent on road and track, the new German generation
also dominated hill climbs. Muller, Auto-Union

to stem the German tide. But to little avail. German
domination was almost total, and even that patriotic
maestro Tazio Nuvolari was now driving for Auto-
Union.

From the German Grand Prix in 1934 to the Yugo-
slav Grand Prix run on the day Britain went to war
with Germany again, the silver Auto-Unions and
Mercedes-Benz fought together with little outside
intervention. But if the honours were retained almost
exclusively by one nation these five years were packed
with technical interest, and with close and magnificent
racing on the grand scale — with great cars that
sounded right. It was, too, a magnificent era for drivers.
A 6 litre Auto-Union in Nurburg's Karussel, a W125
Mercedes in the station hairpin at Monte Carlo,
demanded a blend of muscular and intellectual prowess
which no machine is ever again likely to demand
of its conductor. Is it only nostalgia that leads us to
believe that Rosemeyer, von Brauchitsch and Caracciola, Seaman, Nuvolari and Stuck were fashioned
in an heroic mould that was lost somewhere during
the years of frightfulness that followed this golden era?
Possibly yes — possibly no!

1939

154. From the brilliant Grand Prix products from Stuttgart,
Daimler-Benz derived their little 1½ litre voiturette to deal with
the 158 Alfa Romeos

Champions at the Wheel

Tazio Nuvolari

'The flying Mantuan,' it was said, 'had a pact with the devil.' Many older people who saw him in action claim, even today, that the fiery little Italian, Tazio Nuvolari, was the greatest of them all. That veteran motor racing journalist, W. F. Bradley, who probably saw him win more races than anyone alive, puts him at the head of the list. So do many other authorities. However that may be, he was certainly the most colourful of all the *maestros*, and the most thrilling to watch. He drove with fire and gusto, with such impatience that he would sometimes be seen beating the side panels with one hand even while he was in one of his famous controlled four-wheel slides. And yet he knew how to nurse his cars when the need arose.

In appearance he was light and lithe. His hairy arms, with immensely powerful muscles swelling as he swung the wheel, were one of the sights of between-the-wars racing. He had the dark eyes and olive skin of the true Latin and a lean hatchet face that was often contorted into expressions of frenzy, rage or determination to hold his machine through a corner at a speed that no one else could match.

Nuvolari was born in Mantua in northern Italy on November 16th, 1892. While still in his teens he began his career of speed that lasted almost to his death in 1953 from an illness caused by years of inhalation of fumes. Like so many other fine drivers, he began on motor-cycles, which gave him the timing, and judgement, and above all the remarkably fine degree of balance which in later years allowed him to take his machines to the very limit of adhesion and equilibrium, an acutely dangerous territory explored by few of his contemporaries.

Nuvolari began driving cars like the Ansaldo and Bianchi in the early 1920's with enough skill to be offered the seat of an Alfa Romeo. His exuberance unhappily got the better of him on this occasion, and he ended up in hospital, with no contract. For some time after this he drove a Type 35 Bugatti, with more controlled abandon now — and at last got himself

into the Alfa Romeo team in 1930. There followed nine years of glorious maturity, and glorious spectacle for those who saw him in action. One of his greatest drives, for the R.A.C. Tourist Trophy in 1933, is described later in this book. In the same year he had one of his bitterest combats with his arch-rival Achille Varzi, a smouldering, surly dandy who hated the exuberant Nuvolari. At the Monaco round-the-houses Grand Prix Varzi was in a Bugatti, Nuvolari in his favourite *Scuderia Ferrari* Alfa Romeo — he drove anything that came his way but the Alfa was always his first love. All the great drivers of the day (except Caracciola who had crashed in practice) were there. But from the first lap the race was between the two superbly skilful Italians — Varzi in trim white overalls, Nuvolari in a dirty old yellow sweater. No one else seriously threatened them as, for lap after lap and never more than a few feet apart, first one and then the other led around the winding streets and up and down the hills of the city. Three and a half hours of hub to hub, or nose to tail, motor racing!

There has been no other race like it. One after the other more than half the cars behind them blew up their engines or tore up their transmissions. Two laps to go — Nuvolari leads, and has led for seventeen laps, by a hairsbreadth. Then Varzi slips by accelerating away from the gasworks hairpin. Nuvolari grazes past as they approach the Casino corner, and again Alfa red leads Bugatti blue.

Surely now this must be another triumph for the flying Mantuan? Then next time round, at the same spot, Varzi keeps his Bugatti in third gear until the revs roar past the 7,000 mark. The engine stands it, and the Bugatti has enough speed to creep inches ahead before the corner — and is past again, amid wild cheers from the crowd.

With elbows pumping up and down at every corner, Nuvolari edges up almost alongside the Bugatti, past the station, under the bridge on to the promenade, through the dark tunnel. He almost catches Varzi before the gasometer hairpin, decides to risk all on the

156

Tazio Nuvolari

157

158

1933
156. The Italian wizard's second win at Ulster. His wife congratulates him

1934
157. Plug trouble beset Nuvolari's Bugatti at Monaco. Here he is leading Dreyfus's on the approach to the sharp left-hander along the promenade

1935
158. Although already outclassed by the new German cars, Nuvolari held the lead for 150 kilometres at Montlhéry on June 23rd in his P3 Alfa Romeo. Then transmission trouble put him out of the race

159. By this year Nuvolari had despaired of success with his beloved red Alfas, and had succumbed to the temptations offered by the Germans. Here he is at Donington Park, England, where he won the Grand Prix at 80.49 m.p.h. in the mighty 3 litre V12 rear-engined Auto-Union. The driver is now set back further in the car, and can thus 'aim' the nose in a less awkward manner than in the earlier Auto-Unions

159

Plate 20. At the Swiss Grand Prix at Berne in 1938, the 3 litre Mercedes took the first three places, Caracciola leading Seaman across the line by less than half a minute. It was a rain-swept race, and a disappointing one for Lang, seen here at the first corner after the pits

85

1938

Plate 21. *This superb study of Grand Prix racing in the golden era of the 1930's shows the German driver Manfred von Brauchitsch in his V12-engined Mercedes-Benz at the 1938 Swiss event run at Berne. He took third place behind Caracciola and Seaman*

1956

Plate 22.   G. A. Vandervell, British industrialist, brought colour and success to British motor racing in the late 1950's with his Vanwall cars. Success still lay ahead in 1956. This is Maurice Trintignant at Monte Carlo, at the gasometer hairpin, before his retirement on the 14th lap

1939

160.   Nuvolari at Donington Park again on his race-winning run

161.   Few drivers appeared at ease in the cockpit of the pre-war Auto-Unions; but somehow Nuvolari never looked out of place or in difficulty in any machine

161

winding hill. The engine of his Alfa screams higher and higher. He is going to get by. But no!

Suddenly smoke pours from under his bonnet. An oil pipe has broken, spraying hot oil on to the exhaust, and the Alfa is on fire. Nuvolari ignores it, ignores the waving officials, races on in his crippled machine. The engine fails after the tortuous descent to the promenade, and Nuvolari coasts on. Standing up on his seat ready to jump, he leaps out, and begins to push from behind. All along the sea front the little Italian heaves at the tail of his Alfa, and miraculously reaches his pit amid wild cries from the crowd. Mechanics rush out with extinguishers, and in spite of

Nuvolari's protests that he wants to get to the winning line, halt the machine and spray the engine.

It was all over. Tazio Nuvolari has lost one of his greatest races. But there were, too, the great wins against great odds: the incredible victory in his out-classed Alfa against the entire might of the German Auto-Unions and Mercedes at the Nurburgring. He was victor in all of sixty-two Grands Prix, a dozen of them *grandes epreuves,* in spite of his insistence on driving Italian cars when the Germans were winning almost every race on the calendar. He drove sports cars with equal dash, and he broke records. Driving was his life. He even drove with his leg in plaster after one of his many accidents. Tazio Nuvolari was the greatest spectacle of that spectacular motor racing age, the 1930's.

Richard Beattie Seaman

This Englishman was one of those drivers whose real potentialities were never realized because, like others before him, he was killed at an early age. But he must go down in motor racing history as the greatest British driver before the Second World War, as the first British driver to drive for Mercedes-Benz, and the first British driver to win the German Grand Prix.

At Rugby school his future career was evident to

his closest friends, those who were let into the secret of the forbidden motor-bicycle, which he drove at great speed and with great skill whenever opportunity occurred. His competition career, like that of Tazio Nuvolari, began before he was twenty, in trials and minor events, with an M.G. and a Bugatti. In 1934 he acquired a K3 supercharged M.G. Magnette, the most potent machine the M.G. company ever produced, and raced it in class events all over the Continent. Over the following years he built up a tremendous reputation, especially in $1\frac{1}{2}$ litre racing, mainly with E.R.A.'s and an old Delage which he had rejuvenated until it was almost omnipotent. After he became European champion in this class it was evident that he must progress to the Formula I Grand Prix field, then dominated by Auto-Union and Mercedes-Benz cars, which were more powerful and travelling faster than any cars before or since.

In 1936 Mercedes-Benz had had a disappointing year. For the following season they busied themselves with improving their cars, and reorganizing their team. There was no greater honour at this time than to be invited to drive for the Stuttgart company. Dick Seaman was chosen, and began the most exciting two years of his brief life. In 1937 he held his own, but inexperience with the silver monsters caused him to crash and spend a good deal of time in hospital. The following year he made a magnificent showing, including his victory in the German Grand Prix.

In June 1939 there arrived in Belgium for that country's Grand Prix all the great racing drivers and cars of the day, among them Caracciola, von Brauchitsch, Lang and Seaman on the 3 litre Mercedes, Nuvolari leading the Auto-Unions, backed up by outclassed Delahayes and Alfa Romeos. The road over which they were to fight out one of the last Grands Prix before the German panzers advanced across the nearby frontier was the Spa-Francorchamps circuit, one of the most famous, fastest and most dangerous in Europe. It has always made great demands on drivers as it contains long straights, fast curves on which the best drivers keep their right foot hard down, deceptive corners and gradients, and a 20 m.p.h. hairpin. To these hazards Spa often adds those of mist, fog or pouring rain.

It was raining hard on that June afternoon in 1939 when the great silver German cars were wheeled out on to the circuit on the steep hill by the grandstand and were placed on the leading grid marks. The start was like the opening of a speed-boat race, and the cars were soon lost to sight in their own spray clouds beyond the double bend of Eau Rouge. An Auto-Union was seen to be in the lead when, amid a scream of superchargers, the first cars appeared through the downpour along the tricky fast left-hand bend before La Source. In the lead was Muller's Auto-Union, followed by

Lang's Mercedes, and then Nuvolari in another Auto-Union, dwarfed as always by the huge rear-engined machine he handled with such mastery. They followed one another tightly together through the hairpin by the little inn that gave its name to the slowest part of the circuit.

Seaman was way back in the field at this stage, but the British driver soon settled down to the appalling conditions, and began passing those ahead of him. On the ninth lap the brilliant Caracciola crashed at La Source — the conditions were bad enough for that. Shortly afterwards, one of the Auto-Unions slid uncontrollably off the road.

Seaman fought his way through, soaked to the skin and almost blinded by the driving rain, until he was up with the leaders. And the race speed had climbed to over 94 m.p.h., an incredible pace under these conditions. By the tenth lap, going faster than ever, Seaman had whipped past both the German drivers ahead of him — perhaps the greatest single achievement of his racing career. After a 31-second pit stop the British driver lost the lead momentarily, regained it, and was leading with Lang and Nuvolari behind on the twentieth lap. The rain had eased, but mist had reduced visibility. Pressed hard from behind by his more experienced rivals, this was a terribly

Richard Beattie Seaman

162. First Briton to drive for the Mercedes-Benz works team. Greatest British driver before Stirling Moss

1938

163. Seaman in at the pits during the 1938 German Grand Prix, a splendid victory at 80.75 m.p.h. for the young Englishman

164. Testing at Monza in 1938 before the Italian Grand Prix in his V12 W163 Mercedes-Benz

dangerous time on an extremely dangerous circuit.

Seaman brought his big low Mercedes very fast away from the near-hairpin at Stavelot, and climbed up the valley side through the fast bends. He held his car in a steady slide through Blanchimont, and accelerated away, the spray rising high behind him. He positioned himself for the notorious and very fast left-hander before La Source, got into a slide, and corrected it expertly. But the correction, on the rain-sodden road, had upset the Mercedes's balance. Seaman corrected the other way, began to slide, and lost control.

The silver car seemed to turn once, slid off the road, and hit a pine tree while still going at a great pace.

The car at once burst into flames, and the crash must have knocked out the driver, for when the rescuers arrived Seaman had made no attempt to remove the detachable steering wheel. And no one there knew how to unlock it. Seaman was terribly burned by the time they at last extricated him from the wreckage. They got him to hospital, but he died soon afterwards.

Follow the road from La Source towards Stavelot, and in a few hundred yards you will see a white stone on the verge. It stands in memory of Richard Beattie Seaman — a gallant fighter and a great driver.

Rudolf Caracciola

The name of Rudolf Caracciola will be linked forever with the Mercedes-Benz cars he drove for almost all of his long racing career. 'Rudi', or 'Carach' as many called him, was one of the most liked figures in racing between the wars, whether in hill-climb, record-breaking, sports or Grand Prix machines — all of which he drove with skill and consistency to become the most renowned German driver of his day.

Caracciola first achieved prominence at the wheel of the huge Porsche-designed Mercedes-Benz sports cars of the late 1920's and early 1930's. In these he took on the might of Bentley at the Tourist Trophy

1939

165. *Spa, Belgium. Dick Seaman slides his Mercedes in heavy rain on the Francorchamps circuit, well in the lead. But a few minutes later he lost control on a bend approaching La Source hairpin, his car struck a tree and caught fire. He died soon after*

165

Rudolf Caracciola

166. Greatest German driver

1934

167. 'Rudi' in a P3 Alfa shortly before he re-joined the Mercedes team, for whom he drove with prodigious success until the Second World War broke out five and a half years later

and defeated them. He challenged them again at Le Mans the following year, and succumbed to the weight of numbers. He drove them in stripped form against Alfa Romeo and Bugatti Grand Prix machines. And he entered one in 1930 for the fabulous Mille Miglia, that most remarkable of races, run for a thousand miles half round Italy from 1927 to 1957.

Over winding mountain passes the massive Mercedes seemed to stand small chance of success against the very fast little lithe Alfa Romeos, with men of the calibre of Campari and Nuvolari driving them. Caracciola hoped to make up on the long straights the time lost hurling the brutish Mercedes up and down the mountains, and at one time during the night he held fourth place. That year Nuvolari won at 62.41 m.p.h., seven miles an hour faster than ever before.

But Caracciola brought the big white car back the following year, determined on revenge now that he knew the roads better. Nuvolari replied by bringing to the start at Brescia one of the new straight-eight supercharged 2.3 litre Alfas; it was still a David and Goliath business as the Mercedes, also supercharged, had over 7 litres under its bonnet.

On the long stretch south from Brescia to Bologna Caracciola averaged an incredible 95.8 m.p.h., covering the 129 miles in eight minutes less time than ever before. This was a faster speed than any of the flock of Alfas, driven by the top Italian aces, could hope to match. Morandi in a supercharged O.M. was close behind; then the three top Alfa drivers, Nuvolari, Campari and Borzacchini within seconds of one another. None of them had been able to hold the big white Mercedes on the fast stretches, or through the towns and villages from Brescia. Their chance to gain ground was up and down the mountain passes towards the next stage at Florence. For all his skill and muscular power, Caracciola's lead over the red swarm was cut from nine to five minutes. Tazio Nuvolari was hard on his tail, and the Italian had the advantage of knowing almost every inch of the road back towards Brescia. As the machines roared into

Rome — and there were a hundred of them in the race that year — Nuvolari was in the lead by ninety seconds, and the crowds packed deep along the streets cheered their favourite.

It was dusk. Ahead lay the second crossing of the Apennines, the long climb by the light of the headlamps around hundreds of hairpin bends, straining to the utmost the nerves and the eyes of the drivers; taxing to the utmost the engines, transmission, brakes and the tyres of the cars. Some of the Alfas were having trouble with their tyres. The wild, dashing Arcangeli in the second 2.3 Alfa had made nine tyre changes before Rome, and then switched to another make. But now he achieved an incredibly swift crossing of the mountains down to the Adriatic, and on the road back to Bologna came right back into the picture, and even took the lead, with Campari second and Caracciola third. It seemed as if the German driver had failed again — the gap appeared now too wide to close.

Dawn was just breaking. There was mist hanging close to the ground on the plains, making driving hazardous. But the roads were fast, and they were the sort of roads on which the Mercedes could be pushed right up to its maximum speed of around 115 m.p.h., perhaps a shade more with the supercharger engaged. Not even the 2.3 Alfa could get near these

168.   One of Caracciola's most remarkable feats was to win at
62.84 m.p.h. — the 1931 Mille Miglia in a giant 7 litre 'SSK'
Mercedes-Benz against the full might of the Italian teams. His car
could not have been more unsuitable for the mountain passes,
like the Raticosa, seen here

169. *Thundering into Brescia after his record-breaking 1931 Mille Miglia victory*

170. *And the start of it all, 16 hours, 10 minutes earlier. Caracciola got away seconds later. Soon he was to challenge the might of the Bentley team at Le Mans, but they proved tougher adversaries than the Italian Alfas and O. M. s*

speeds. Caracciola drove flat out to Treviso, eating up the miles as the sun rose over the plains.

This is how W. F. Bradley saw the end of this race in Brescia, sixteen hours after the start:

Sunday morning broke brilliantly. By six o'clock the Corso Venezia was packed with spectators, the great majority of whom had spent the night in the cafés and public squares of the town, following the progress of the cars on the illuminated scoreboards. A trumpet call, a waving of a flag down the Corso, and a thousand people were pressed against the railings, and as many pairs of eyes were strained to catch a glimpse of the oncoming car. It was the white Mercedes, still with Caracciola at the wheel, for he had driven the entire thousand miles.

It was a magnificent victory for the young, chubby-faced German driver — and it was not for another quarter century that Mercedes-Benz again successfully challenged the Italians in their own special race, the Mille Miglia.

But only three years later, with the coming of the 750 kg. formula and the new generation of Mercedes Grand Prix cars, the Italians had to yield supremacy in Grand Prix racing. And leading the German drivers past the chequered flag again and again was Rudi Caracciola, Germany's most successful driver of all time, who died in 1959 at the age of fifty-eight years.

Wilbur Shaw

The greatest Indianapolis driver was a sturdy, dark-haired, handsome man with a pencil-thin moustache, a self-confident manner, a warm heart, and an enthusiasm for the Speedway equalled only by his record of successes on it. Wilbur Shaw began racing at the brickyard in 1927, placed fourth that year (no mean feat for a rookie). He placed second in 1933 and 1935, and won outright in 1937, 1939 and 1940. He survived all the Speedway's hazards to become its manager,

1963

Plate 23.   The Branson and Hurtubise duel

Plate 24.   The cockpit of Dan Gurney's Lotus

1963

Plate 25.   Thompson-Harvey Aluminum Special

1964

Plate 26.   Front suspension detail

Plate 27.   The Ford engine of Jim Clark's Lotus

Wilbur Shaw

171. One of Indy's most loved characters — and surely the greatest driver ever to race at the brickyard

1937
172. The start of the 1937 race, Shaw's first victory

only to die in an air crash in 1954.

Shaw was already marked as a likely future winner in 1936 after his close second places in the two previous years. He had built his own car, an ultra-aerodynamic machine powered by the perennial 4-cylinder 'Offy'. It proved its speed by holding the lead at 200 miles by some eighty seconds — and demonstrated its imperfect preparation when the bonnet rivets began to work loose, and he was forced to retire.

Shaw later took this car to challenge the European road racing machines at Roosevelt Raceway, but could do nothing against them and crashed. But the Shaw-Gilmore Special, as he named it, was fast enough

to take the lead at Indy the following year and hold it. Still with thirty laps to go, Shaw began to lose oil pressure, and regulations forbade him from topping up. He nursed his car with beautifully calculated restraint, deliberately losing six seconds a lap to the second man, and even allowing him to nose ahead on the very last lap.

It was the closest finish to the 500 ever. The crowd was really getting a superb spectacle, and showing its appreciation by leaping and shouting in a fever of excitement. Then Shaw put his foot hard down for the first time for nearly an hour, and eased ahead. He won by just two seconds!

The same car was still fast enough to qualify well in 1938, but not fast enough to win. Shaw shrewdly turned to Italy for his next mount, an 8CTF Maserati, described earlier in this book. More than a minute behind with seventy laps to go, Shaw demonstrated his mastery of the brickyard, driving relentlessly and yet with superb control. He made first place with forty miles left, and held it to the end.

As a two-time winner, Shaw was now among the aristocrats of Indianapolis. The following year he sailed home again, the first man ever to win in two successive years.

Wilbur Shaw came close to beating even this superb record in 1941, still in the big 8-cylinder Maserati. He was in such a strong position with the race three-quarters run that no sane man there would give anyone else an outside chance. This time fate stepped in, in the odd way it will in motor racing. One of his wheels had been imperfectly balanced for the race. Shaw's pit knew this, and marked it with chalk, indicating that it should be used only in an emergency. But before the race there had been a fire in the pits, and the firemen's hose water had washed off that warning sign. It was Shaw's misfortune, that was to cost him the race, much prize money, and an even more special place in Indy history, that this wheel was put on his car during a stop. The wheel broke

on the south-west turn, and the Maserati crashed immediately, injuring Shaw.

Wilbur Shaw never raced at the Speedway again. But he remained associated with it, managing it with skill and enterprise to the day of his death.

173. 174. 175. Three shots of Wilbur Shaw with his Maserati that gave him the chequered flag in 1939 and 1940, and made a sensation at Indianapolis. The 8-cylinder Italian car could not match the German machines in European racing but proved reliable and fast in Shaw's masterly hands

173

Where's that Engine?

Once upon a time there was a Grand Prix car with its engine behind the driver, and most people laughed when they beheld it. It was made by a magician called Dr Rumpler, who waved his wand wonderfully over mechanical things. Nobody believed that it would work properly, but the magician did not mind. He loved his strange motor car and christened it *Tropfenwagen*, which means 'shaped like a drop of falling water'. And then very soon it vanished, and the poor magician died. But lo! Forty years passed and the magician's ghost came back to the Grand Prix circuits and laughed mightily to see that all the motor-cars were now *Tropfenwagen* with their engines behind the driver. And therein lies a moral — indeed several morals!

The earliest horseless carriages had all been rear-engined and over the years engineers have experimented with putting the driver in front of his source of power. But the first rumblings of the revolution that has led today to every ultra-performance automobile being rear-engined emanated from Dr Rumpler of the Benz motor works in Germany in 1923. His 6-cylinder, twin-cam, lightweight, completely aerodynamic Grand Prix car was never fully developed.

Ten years later, however, it provided the inspiration for the massive Auto-Union. Then in 1945 Charles Cooper, a fifty-two-year-old British engineer, who owned a garage at Surbiton in south London, and had had extensive experience with high performance cars between the wars, started the Cooper Car Company. At the same time he re-introduced a trend begun by Dr Rumpler and perpetuated by Dr Ferdinand Porsche's Auto-Union.

The Cooper saga began with a crude surgical operation. Impressed by the road-holding, light weight and simplicity of the little Fiat 500 'Topolino', he took two of them, cut their frames in half, and welded together two rear parts. He then placed a driving seat and the controls at the front, and an air-cooled single cylinder motor-bicycle engine at the rear. It proved to be the ideal mount for the young drivers —

176. 177. Was this 'the Daddy of them all'? Dr Rumpler, of aero-engine fame, produced this remarkably aerodynamic and technically advanced machine for the 1923 European Grand Prix at Monza

1947

178. Eric Brandon with the original rear-engined Cooper

179. 180. 181. After the 1934—1939 rear-engined Auto-Union exercise, the Grand Prix car conformed to tradition in the 1940's and 1950's with a forward mounted engine driving the rear wheels. Here are three random examples — 158/9 Alfa Romeo; Vanwall Special and its Ferrari-engined ancestor the Thin Wall Special on the grid at Goodwood; nad 1½ litre supercharged Ferrari

182. But in the early 1960's, the engine-behind-the-driver arrangement re-established itself. Cooper (seen here) pioneered, and one by one all others conformed

183. *Cooper-Climax with prototype V8 engine, at Silverstone for testing shortly before competing in the 1961 German Grand Prix*

184. *April 1952 Moss and the 500 c.c. Kieft Norton winning the Earl of March Trophy at Goodwood, averaging 78.07 m. p. h.*

1923

185. *Superb study of advanced thinking almost half a century ago. Six cylinders, two overhead camshafts, two carburettors, roller bearings and aluminium pistons. Rear-engined Benz with strut-mounted external radiator*

like Stirling Moss — working their way into the new Formula III 5oo c.c. racing. So superior were the Coopers in this class of racing that after a few years they had almost no competition.

From these beginnings Charles Cooper and his son John spread out into other fields — into Formula II racing and into sports cars, and even into Grand Prix racing. The Cooper-Bristol in the hands of Mike Hawthorn on several occasions frightened the Italians, and led to Hawthorn being invited to drive for Ferrari. A few years later a young Australian named Jack Brabham suggested to the Coopers that the same Bristol engine at the rear, matched with their lightweight

sports chassis, might be fast enough for $2\frac{1}{2}$ litre Formula I racing. This machine had little success against the bigger engined Grand Prix cars of the day, but it proved the genesis for the 1957 Formula II Coventry-Climax engined racing car, which in its turn was developed and enlarged to carry first a 2 litre, then a 2.2 litre and finally a full $2\frac{1}{2}$ litre engine. This highly sophisticated Cooper—now a far cry from the elementary '500' of earlier years — challenged the Ferrari, Maserati, Vanwall and other big contenders in Grand Prix racing in the late 1950's.

The Grand Prix Cooper had its first success in South America in the hands of Stirling Moss. Maurice Trin-

186.   A view of the 'sawn off' back of the Cooper-Climax being driven by Ivor Bueb at speed on the Dunrod circuit N. Ireland during the T. T. race in 1955

187.   Popular cars of the time were the 500 c.c. J.A.P. engined Coopers; there were 43 entries in the 500 Club meeting at the Brands Hatch circuit, September 1950

1959

188. 189. 190. After the early efforts of Doctors Rumpler and Porsche, it was the Coopers (father and son) who set the pattern again; and it was from their 1½ litre Formula II car of the late 1950's that there stemmed the rear-engine revolution of the 1960's

tignant, the last of the great French drivers, confirmed its potential at Monte Carlo. And suddenly, in a whirlwind conquest that left the opposition gasping, the Cooper — light, whippy, tenacious, superbly balanced — had conquered all the great racing circuits of Europe. In 1959 and 1960 Coopers won the Manufacturers' Championship, in the hands of Jack Brabham in both years, who gained for himself at the same time the World Championship of Drivers.

Imitators soon appeared. Ferrari, Lotus, B.R.M., all conformed to the rear-engine layout and learnt much also from the Coopers' theories on chassis design. Soon the Cooper no longer automatically ran away with every event. But since 1958 its influence on design has been so profound that it is no exaggeration to say that it has entirely changed the face of motor racing. And not only in Europe. As described earlier, it was responsible for the end of the traditional American roadster, and the beginning of a new technological era at the Indianapolis Speedway.

You can reasonably argue that Dr Rumpler started all this more than forty years ago, and that Dr Porsche also helped create the modern rear-engined racing car. But it was the Coopers, father and son, who elaborated and refined and perfected the basic arrangement of the driver and his engine. Their influence will be seen for many years to come.

1958

191. Roy Salvadori was one of the staunchest disciples of the rear-engine religion, and time and again he proved that good balance and light weight could offset any power handicap. Here he is coming in second in his Cooper at the International Trophy

1961

192. World Champion Jack Brabham, Cooper designer and race manager John Cooper — two men who have done so much for British motor racing prestige, usually with a smile!

Maestro Moss

1948

193. Young Moss, already showing promise

194. Moss fulfilling all that had ever been expected of him twelve years later. Here he is at Monaco in 1960, in Rob Walker's rear-engined Lotus, on the way to victory by fifty-two seconds over McLaren's Cooper

On a May day in 1948, when you couldn't buy a car and weren't allowed to buy petrol, a very young and eager boy was seen with a very small racing machine at the bottom of a hill in Gloucestershire. The boy's name was Stirling Moss, his car was one of the early Coopers described in the last chapter, and at eighteen he was off on his first motor race — against the clock. Until his two practice runs Moss had never seen Prescott Hill before. He had driven his Cooper a total distance of about ten miles. He was up against experienced drivers. And he appeared to be quite unperturbed by the whole business!

When his number was called, Moss came to the line in the spotless cream Cooper, the flag fell — and he was away. A minute later the loud-speakers announced a time of 50.01 seconds, a new class record. Others did better later, and Moss had to be content with fourth place in the 500 c.c. class. But there were one or two people there on that sunny afternoon who recognized that they might be in the presence of potential genius. There had been a certain manner, a certain style, and a degree of restained enthusiasm about young Moss's runs up Prescott Hill that hinted in this direction. There was further evidence next month. At Stanmer near Brighton he won by a wide margin. 'Young Moss,' wrote *The Autocar*, 'with his first real racing car put up two terrific climbs and

196

1948

195. 196. Zestful, exuberant Moss at Stanmer Park hillclimb in 1948. At his second-ever motoring competition, his father opposite had said, 'Here's your chance!' And young Stirling took it. He clocked 58.78 seconds to win the 500 c.c. class

beat the field . . .'

Among those who knew Moss personally, who knew his family background, and understood his personality, the future of 'S. Moss, promising newcomer' was even easier to predict. In the multitude of determining factors that go to make up a great motor racing driver, many important ones were in his favour even before he put his foot on the accelerator — and this he did at an earlier age than most of us. Not only had his mother been a prominent rally driver before the war, but his father, Alfred Moss, had mixed racing — including Indianapolis — with his profession as a dentist. So the competitive instinct, as well as an

1960

197. *The veteran in command*

198. *The newcomer is wished good luck by his veteran racing driver father. Stirling at Silverstone in 1948, the year of his first successes*

enthusiasm for mechanics, were a part of his inheritance. And there were numerous occasions on horseback, from his earliest childhood, that not only nourished this competitive urge but also sharpened his natural sense of balance and timing, and taught him the need for concentration and self-control. Never has chance had less to do with the making of a racing driver: no chance factor deflected the course of his career. Moss was barely in his teens when he announced his final decision about his future — 'I thought I'd have a go at being a racing driver.' From that time the ambition became an obsession, to the exclusion of everything else.

199. Formula III 500 c.c. racing, schooling ground for so many new drivers in the 1940's and 1950's, offered young Moss the opportunity to win his spurs. This he did with predictable frequency, sometimes in a Cooper-Norton

This was the beginning of an unprecedented career in motor racing that was to last for fourteen years. It is possible to claim that others have handled Grand Prix cars with equal skill and courage; that one or two drivers have driven sports cars as well and as successfully (though it is hard to think of their names); and that he might have had a hard time beating a certain Swede and a few others in rallies, that ... But these claims cannot withstand the undeniable truth that the world has never seen, and is unlikely to see again in our lifetime, an all-round driver combining the speed, tenacity, subtlety, bravery and understanding of tactics and the whole world of motor racing

as did Stirling Moss.

It is now more than four years since he was seen behind the wheel, and a new generation is growing up to whom the name is something of a legend. There may be some who do not understand the real paradox of his career — that Stirling Moss was never World Champion. But there is one clue to this extraordinary fact in a single important facet of his complex character. He preferred to drive British cars, and for much of his long career he competed against machines that were both faster and more reliable than his own. For example, back in 1948, after a series of hill-climb wins, he found himself on the starting line at the

202. John Cooper, plug spanner at the ready, has last words with Stirling Moss at Goodwood before a minor event in 1950. Observe front-engined car!

201. He also drove a Cooper—J.A.P.

203. In the year before he was invited to join the Mercedes team in 1955, Moss drove a D-type Jaguar in the Tourist Trophy in Northern Ireland

200. By 1950, Moss was almost unchallengeable in 500 c.c. racing. Here he is at Brands Hatch

Brighton Speed Trials in a machine that was quite outclassed. Some of the Cooper 500 drivers had managed to acquire Norton in place of J.A.P. engines, and on the straight line of the Madeira Drive where driving skill consisted largely of putting your foot hard down, Moss was left behind.

In Grand Prix racing, which he eagerly joined, he was to experience time and again the frustration of driving underpowered machines, and for season after season, in H.W.M.'s, E.R.A.'s, Connaughts, Cooper-Altas's, the best he could do was to demonstrate his superior skill in adversity — a whole heart-breaking series of David-and-Goliath combats in which Goliath always conquered.

Meanwhile, when he was given the best, he showed that there was no one who could stay with him — at the Tourist Trophy, for example, where he won two years in succession for Jaguar. For six years he accumulated Gold Stars, silver cups, and firsts and honours by the score, until in Britain he became that curious and mysterious figure, 'the household word'. His name was everywhere. Even if he failed to win, this was news. He sponsored advertisements, put his name to articles in newspapers and magazines, wrote books, was quoted and misquoted — became the personification of speed.

By 1954, with great reluctance, he bought a new 250F/1 Maserati, and at last showed what he could do with a top-class Formula I racing car. At the Italian Grand Prix, for example, he fought his way through all the great drivers of the day, slip-streamed Fangio, got by, and led comfortably. Then with twelve laps to go his oil tank split, and he had to push his car home — amid the cheers of a sympathetic crowd. Moss notched up major victories during his first season with his Maserati. But this was also the year of the return to racing of Mercedes-Benz — and this alone meant that there was once again a full team of faster machines than his own on the Grand Prix circuits. However, his driving was so fast and cool, his judgement so superior, that he was invited to drive for the German factory in 1955. And at last, at long last, he had a Formula I car that was not only as fast, but superior in almost every respect to those of any other team.

To accept an invitation to drive for Mercedes-Benz is also — as Dick Seaman had discovered seventeen years earlier — to accept the rigid discipline of Stuttgart, represented by the formidable sergeant-major-like figure of Alfred Neubauer. Moss was prepared for all this, and prepared to stick rigidly to team orders, which included playing second fiddle to Juan Manuel Fangio, the reigning World Champion. What the finishing order of the Grands Prix of 1955 would have been had Moss not been under restraint from Neubauer is a fruitless speculation. A good number of people have said that Moss was fractionally a faster driver; Moss himself has always modestly denied this. The table of records for 1955 gives the British driver credit for only one *grande épreuve*, the British Grand Prix, which he won by a hairsbreadth from the Argentinian. But it also starkly states the result of the Mille Miglia thus:

First: Stirling Moss Mercedes-Benz SLR 10 hrs 7 mins 48 secs (97.93 m.p.h.)

Second: Juan Fangio Mercedes-Benz SLR 10 hrs 39 mins 35 secs

Behind these figures is concealed a race that is usually regarded as the most hazardous, the most heroic, the most skilful and spectacular ever won by the world's greatest all-round driver. The situation was a close parallel with the 1931 event when Caracciola's Mercedes was hounded all the way by hordes of Alfa Romeos. In 1955 the Mercedes team was there in strength, but the defending side had enormous power in the shape of Maseratis and Ferraris — the latter in 3.8 litre and even 4.4 litre form, against the Mercedes' 3 litres. The Mille Miglia had also grown mighty over the years, with over 500 entries, ranging from tiny Fiats and French D.B.'s. For the Italians, national prestige was at stake; the foreign invasion must be repelled! The Germans

204

114

1956

204. When he finally and reluctantly 'went foreign' after many seasons of frustration with British cars, often produced on a shoestring budget, Moss chose the Italian Maserati. Here he is in his 250/F1

1962

Plate 28. A Ferrari year — but not at Monte Carlo! Phil Hill fought vainly in his '120-degree' V6 Ferrari against McLaren's Cooper, crossing the line 1.6 seconds behind after two hours, forty-six minutes racing!

28

29

205. Peerless drive — the historic 1955 Mille Miglia, when Moss broke every record, and every Italian heart, in his German Mercedes

1957

Plate 29. Fangio and Moss locked in combat on the first lap of the 1957 Monaco Grand Prix. Two laps later Moss, in the lead in the green Vanwall, overdid it at the chicane, and Fangio went on to victory

Plate 30. Fangio and Moss, all smiles!

1961

Plate 31. Four years later, with Fangio in retirement, Moss made no mistake around the Monte Carlo circuit, and triumphed in his Lotus against the full might of the faster Ferrari team

were equally intent on crushing the opposition.

For a whole day the countryside and villages and towns — and the city of Rome itself — shuddered under the aural impact, as this battery of racing cars tore through Ravenna, Ancona and Pescara, from Rome to Florence and back towards Brescia, hurling up the mountain passes, and down a series of dangerous hairpins to the valleys below. The world will never again see spectacles like those last Mille Miglias!

At Ravenna the dashing, handsome Castellotti led in his 4.4 litre Ferrari at almost 120 m.p.h. Moss was two minutes behind, with his bearded navigator Denis Jenkinson signalling by hand code the nature of the corners and hazards that lay ahead, conversation being impossible above the scream of the straight-eight Mercedes engine. At Ancona Castellotti had slipped back, Moss had taken the lead, with the wily, experienced Taruffi seconds behind. By Pescara the Italian had taken over the lead, and it was Ferrari — Mercedes — Mercedes — Mercedes — Mercedes, Fangio running fifth. But Moss fought back, and streaked into Rome less than ten seconds ahead of the Ferrari.

And so the ding-dong battle went on, while behind the leaders the price for this unprecedented speed was being paid. There were crashes — Moss himself did some denting! — and mechanical failures by the score,

of both German and Italian cars. But by Florence no one could stay with the flying Moss, and he led back all the way to Brescia, averaging close to the 100-mark, nearly ten miles an hour faster than the Mille Miglia had ever been run before. It was the most incredible achievement of an amazing career.

With the retirement from racing of Mercedes-Benz, Moss returned to Maserati for the 1956 season, winning in Italy and Monaco. Then he switched to Vanwall, a British Grand Prix car that had been showing increasing promise. He applied himself with single-minded dedication to winning the World Championship, driving British; some people thought with too much single-mindedness. He was a very serious young man, very conscious of his responsibilities, very conscious that chance had too often prevented him from reaching the summit of the motor racing world, and that there was a new generation of extremely fast young men appearing around him on the grid — some showing tremendous potential. How long would he be able to stay with them? When would his cars stop breaking? The Vanwall was terribly quick, but a shade frail for Moss in his most determined mood. The Championship could well have been his in 1958 had he not acted as a witness in Hawthorn's support over a re-starting incident. The relaxed, beer-drinking, pipe-smoking Mike, and Moss at his most tense, ran neck and neck

that year, and Hawthorn won — by a single point — perhaps because he didn't much care.

Moss's morale suffered another blow with the break-up of his marriage. In 1959 his fortunes seemed at their lowest ebb. Then he teamed up with R.R.C. 'Rob' Walker, the whiskey millionaire who ran a racing team as a hobby. It was a splendid combination. The two men got on well, and with the loss of his ambition to become first British World Champion, and a general emotional reappraisal, Moss began to enjoy life again. But as in Moss's years as an independent, this private *équipe* naturally could not acquire the very latest cars from the factories, which were running their own teams; and once again this handicap told against him. Right up to his final accident in 1962, the Championship continued to elude him, although this period was marked by some of his most magnificent drives, one of which is described in the next chapter.

The British soldier, it is said, is at his best in adversity. Not everyone will agree with this. But no one will deny that Stirling Moss was at his most magnificent when all the odds of chance and fate were stacked against him.

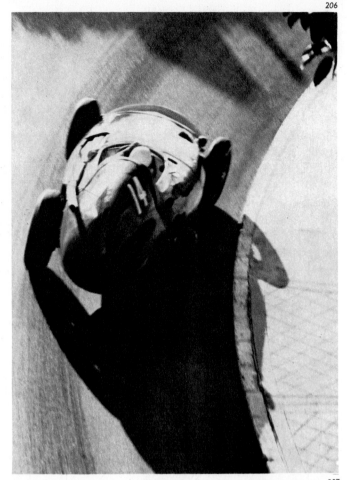

1956, 1957

206. 207. Whether he was at the wheel of one of the last 'big bangers' left or the new generation of lightweight 'back-enders', Moss revealed relaxed class and style which we may never see again. Below here he is with Vanwalls at Monaco

1959

208. Practice at Silverstone in preparation for the big International motor race meeting organized by the British Racing Drivers' Club. Here Stirling Moss is pushed away from the pits at Silverstone during practice

209. At Aintree with the tumultuous 4-cylinder 1959 B.R.M.

210. Moss with the FI Cooper-B.R.M., again at Aintree

208

209

210

Epic Duels

The Tourist Trophy is Britain's oldest motor race, although today it is a pathetic shadow of its former years of greatness. It was first run round the Isle of Man back in 1905, and in those early years it really was for 'touring' cars. In later years, stripped racing machines were allowed. Then in 1928 it was revived on a magnificent road circuit outside Belfast in Ireland. The regulations were tightened up, and only sports cars were permitted. By 1933, although by no means a Grand Prix, the definition of 'sports car' had been stretched so that mudguards were not obligatory and superchargers were fitted to most of the cars. The race consisted of thirty-five laps of a winding circuit

$3\frac{2}{3}$ miles long, and the complex handicapping system gave the smallest cars an advantage of about three and a half laps.

The year 1933 was the finest of all the vintage M. G. seasons, and there were no less than a dozen entered for the T.T., with 2.3 Alfa Romeos and 1,100 c.c. and $1\frac{1}{2}$ litre Rileys as main opposition. Two new M.G. models had appeared earlier in the year, that hectic little terror the J4 supercharged Midget, and the 1,100 c.c. K3 Magnette, also supercharged, and with an epicyclic Wilson gearbox. The K3 Magnette had a performance about equal to that of an M.G.B. of today; the smaller 750 c.c. car was a good deal more

211. 'The flying Mantuan', Tazio Nuvolari, the fierce, wiry, muscular Italian, one of the greatest drivers of all time

212. Start of the 1933 T. T. The unsupercharged $1\frac{1}{2}$ litre Rileys and the 'blown' 1,100 M. G. s get away together. Eyston and Whitcroft are in the leading Rileys; the eventual winner is number 17

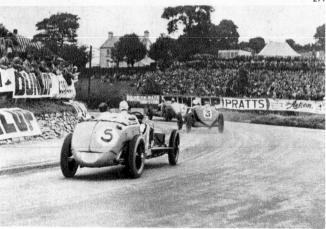

213. Quarry Corner. Nuvolari (17) comes through behind Hailwood's Midget and Hall's Magnette

Driver: Tazio Nuvolari
Race: R.A.C. Tourist Trophy
Car: K3 M.G. Magnette
Date: September 1933

accelerative than the current Midget — and also vastly rougher.

Tazio Nuvolari had been tempted over from Italy to drive one of the K3 M. G.'s, and he took to it (in spite of its unfamiliar gearbox) as if it had been an Alfa. Among those who were driving the little J4 Midgets was H.C. 'Hammy' Hamilton, one of the fieriest Irishmen ever to get behind a racing wheel.

In the early stages of the race these two M.G. exponents were threatened by one or two of the more skilful drivers, including that daring little genius, Freddie Dixon, who always persuaded more power out of his Rileys than was decent. But soon the T. T.

settled down to a furious duel between Hamilton and Nuvolari, with the Italian fighting to reduce his handicap. But in a long race like this a lot depended on the pit stops. This is how Hamilton appeared at a crucial stage of the battle:

At two o'clock he came charging in and at once began throwing away the race. Never calm or untemperamental, he shouted instructions at his mechanic, who responded the wrong way and became more hamfisted as Hamilton became angrier. Fuel was thrown everywhere, the filler cap left undone, it took a minute to raise the front axle. Then the starter failed, the bonnet was opened up

214. *Nuvolari, great Alfa lover, chose to drive British, and trounced the British-driven Alfas of Earl Howe, the Hon. Brian Lewis and Tim Rose-Richards, seen here in that order at Quarry*

215. *The J4 blown M.G. Midgets proved incredibly fast on the twisty Ards circuit. This is J. L. Ford at Dundonald, with Nuvolari pressing him hard*

again while the mechanic did his best to use a spanner as a switch, succeeding only in setting alight to his petrol-sodden gloves and overalls with a spark from the terminals. The poor man was now in such a state that he could not buckle the bonnet strap and . . . well, in all it was nearly seven minutes before a furious Hammy was away. Nuvolari took full advantage of his opponent's delay. Those who were there said they had never seen the winding, dangerous Ards circuit lapped like it. Once he just grazed a telegraph pole, but otherwise his timing and precision were faultless. Up went his lap speed, to an incredible 81 m.p.h. Hamilton replied furiously with 75.77 m.p.h. in his smaller car — again a lap record for his class, by a wide margin.

Two laps to go. There were only seconds between the two M.G.'s. Could the wild Irishman hold his slim lead? The tiny M.G. was flying round the circuit — he might make it.

And he probably would have done. But suddenly his mechanic glanced at the fuel gauge. It was registering zero. They could never manage another fifteen miles. At the beginning of the last lap, with the crowd of nearly half a million on its feet, the supercharged J4 Midget tore into its pit. This time there was no delay. Hammy threw in a single can of petrol, and

216. *The fiery Irishman, H. C. Hamilton, fought with Nuvolari all the way. He lapped the sinuous 13¾-mile circuit at over 75 m.p.h. — not bad for 750 c.c. nearly 35 years ago!*

217. *Tim Rose-Richards (blown 2.3 Alfa) passes Chris Staniland's 1½ Riley. Note spectator control. No wonder the series ended in disaster three years later*

218. *George Eyston pushes his Riley fast through Comber. This is real road racing*

219. *Clipping inches and seconds — Nuvolari style. 'He was as safe as houses,' remarked his riding mechanic, Alec Hounslow, after it was all over*

220. *Dry road, sun out, crowd cheering, flag falling, Hounslow acknowledging. The great moment, after nearly six hours racing. Wonderful car, wonderful driver, wonderful race*

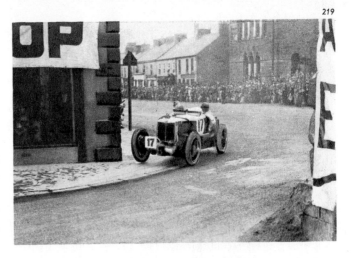

they were away again in twenty seconds, supercharger screaming.

But Nuvolari had gone by, his mechanic Alec Hounslow ('He was as safe as houses,' he said of Nuvolari afterwards) holding on tight. He had just switched on to reserve fuel after the Italian had raised his hand from the wheel in despair, as the engine coughed. Now they had enough to make it, with a few seconds to spare, if nothing went wrong. Nuvolari made no mistakes. He had fallen in love with the eager, responsive M.G. during the race, and he was not going to wreck it on this last lap. And yet the outcome depended on seconds. Down winding Bradshaw's Brae, into Newtownards, a very sharp right-hander past the grey town hall, and on to the long straight with the dials showing 6,500 r.p.m. and 115 m.p.h. Through Comber village, brushing against the wall of the famous butcher's shop and on towards Dundonald . . . Nuvolari and Hounslow bent hard over in their seats at the hairpin, then there was little more than a mile to go. The chequered flag fell. It was all over, and Nuvolari had made it by just forty seconds — winning for the second time Britain's greatest motor race.

Driver: **Juan Manuel Fangio**
Race: **German Grand Prix**
Car: **Maserati 250/F**
Date: **August 1957**

221. Fangio, the inscrutable, indestructable Argentinian. For a decade he was one of the dominant figures in Grand Prix racing. During his finest years, no one could drive a racing car faster

222. He drove many makes, preferred Grand Prix to sports cars, preferred the 2½ litre Maserati above all others

This is a very short story, not about a whole motor race, nor about a racing driver's career, but about the last few laps of one of the last races won by the most successful Grand Prix driver of recent years — some say of all time.

Juan Manuel Fangio is now safely retired from racing, a rich, stoutish, middle-aged man running a highly successful automobile business in his native Argentine. For all but his earliest years after he came to Europe, he was almost unbeatable, and won the World Championship more often than anyone before or since.

In 1957 he was in his last full season of racing.

He had seen challengers come and go, he had seen men retire, and others die. He was a true veteran. And like many another veteran he was all too conscious of the new, promising young stars in the motor racing firmament. Among them were Luigi Musso of Italy, an extremely fast driver for Enzo Ferrari, and two gay young fair-haired Englishmen, Peter Collins and Mike Hawthorn, close friends who also drove under the famous insignia of the flying horse. Although Fangio had often driven Ferraris, in his last seasons he preferred the Maserati, and it was in this car that he had pinned his faith in his attempt to retain the World Championship for the fifth time.

The Nurburgring is a long 14.2-mile circuit that winds and climbs and falls again in mountainous, wooded country in western Germany. Most of the 1957 German Grand Prix was an uninspiring procession, with Fangio far out in front, Hawthorn and Collins keeping station behind. One reason why the Argentinian had pulled out such a big lead was made clear when Fangio came into his pit — not in trouble but for fuel. He had started with a half empty tank, which had given him a great advantage over the Ferraris in the early stages. His Maserati was stationary for almost a minute while petrol was pumped in, and during that time the two big British-driven Ferraris roared by. When Fangio got in and accelerated away there were twelve laps of the race left, and he was about fifty seconds behind. He had five seconds a lap to make up to win!

It did not seem impossible, remembering past displays by the champion. But Fangio was now forty-six years old, the two British drivers were no longer novices — one was to be World Champion himself the next year — and they were at the top of their form. In fact, on the very next lap, Collins, running second to Hawthorn, put in a record of 9 minutes, 28.9 seconds, and soon passed him. At the same time Fangio was suddenly seen to be travelling very fast indeed — faster than anyone else on the circuit. He made up five seconds on that same lap. Then Hawthorn

1957

Plate 32. *Besides his magnificent Nurburgring victory, Fangio demonstrated his supreme prowess all over Europe this year. At Monaco, he slipped imperturbably through the wreckage of the cars of Collins, Hawthorn and Moss in his Maserati after the famous multiple crash, and remained serenely in command until the flag fell*

32

34

1965

Plate 34. *Promising newcomer Denis Hulme at Clermont-Ferrand*

Plate 35. *Jack Stewart in the French Grand Prix*

1962

Plate 33. Lorenzo Bandini shared Ferrari's year of triumph.
Here he is at Monaco

1965

Plate 36. Another Flying Scotsman. Jackie Stewart appears destined for the highest honours in motor racing. Here he demonstrates style and verve at Zandvoort

Plate 37. Lotus conductor Jackie Stewart busily dealing with fractions of seconds to secure a good grid position for the German Grand Prix

37

223. *These two pictures sum up the desperate nature of Fangio's pursuit during the closing stages of the race. Here he is, far above the limit*

224. *At the same time Mike Hawthorn and Peter Collins struggle to hold their Ferraris in the lead*

put on steam, whipped past his friend, and came past the grandstands a length ahead of him.

Nine more minutes passed. Two smudges of red appeared from down the long straight. Collins was ahead again — just. But this time little more than half a minute went by before the long-snouted snarling Maserati raced into view. Nine seconds gain on one lap! It was scarcely possible. But at this rate the Champion would catch the Ferraris before the last lap. From twenty seconds Fangio reduced the gap to fifteen, then to nine.

The crowd was on its feet, roaring encouragement. Fangio responded with a 90.54 m.p.h. lap — an unattainable speed round the 'ring', people had said. At the end of the twentieth lap Hawthorn came through, and almost in the same blast of sound Peter Collins in the sister Ferrari. And where was Fangio? What had happened to the Champion? People looked in vain far down the straight, glanced back at the two Ferraris, and suddenly realized that the Maserati was right with the two British-driven cars. He had knocked eleven seconds off Hawthorn's lead, was right on Collins' tail, had put up the all-time record to 91.84 m.p.h. The man was fantastic — he was *vom Teufel besessen*, 'possessed by the devil himself'!

Before they were into the Karussel behind the pits Fangio was past Collins, his rear wheels sending up

a stone that smashed the Briton's goggles. And then he was after Hawthorn, still going like a hurricane. He caught him before the lap was completed: there was nothing, absolutely nothing, that Mike could do about it. He tried to hold the Maserati, of course. But it was a hopeless cause with Fangio in this fanatical state.

There were many present at the Nurburgring who had seen the Argentinian champion vanquish the enemy before, with uncanny skill and a perfection of style. But none had witnessed anything like this. It was an achievement that will never be forgotten by this great driver's admirers. It also ensured for Juan Manuel his fifth World Championship, and provided a fitting climax to his last full season of racing.

225. Fangio takes Peter Collins behind the pits/grandstand area, a rear wheel throwing up a stone that broke a lens of Collins's goggles, and is already closing on Mike Hawthorn

Britain had her back to the wall in 1961, the first season of a new formula restricting engine capacity to a mere $1\frac{1}{2}$ litres. After a period of dominance with the old $2\frac{1}{2}$ litre limit, British constructors were aghast at the proposal to cut engine size, and protested that the new regulations were retrograde and would lack spectator appeal. While the British argued, Enzo Ferrari's team busied themselves modifying the new cars (rear-engined at last!) and new engines which had been competing in $1\frac{1}{2}$ litre Formula II events in the previous season. So at the beginning of 1961, while Ferrari had his cars right and his drivers (the German Wolfgang von Trips, and Americans

226. Nine kilometres later he nipped past the second Englishman, to lead on the 21st lap — and confirm his fifth World Championship. His average over the 22 laps was 88.79 m.p.h.

Phil Hill and Richie Ginther) bursting with self-confidence, the British teams were unprepared, since they were not due to get their new engines until late in the season.

Against this formidable Italian line-up with machines of 180 to 190 h.p., the British mustered outclassed 4-cylinder cars with an output of only around 150 h.p., and the Germans (in the shape of Porsche) interesting but equally underpowered machines. Once again this year Stirling Moss was driving for the private *équipe* of Rob Walker. He understood perfectly how the dice were loaded against him and his Lotus that was giving away some 30% in power to the red Ferraris.

Driver: Stirling Moss
Race: Monaco Grand Prix
Car: 1½ litre Lotus-Climax
Date: May 1961

227. 228. 229. All Stirling Moss's virtuosity and courage is demonstrated in these pictures of him holding off — by split seconds much of the time — the assault of the more powerful and faster Ferraris

228

229

On his side Moss possessed more motor racing wisdom than anyone else in the Principality, going back some thirteen years, an unsurpassed knowledge of the circuit (hadn't he raced round-the-houses here in the 1940's when he was still an unknown novice?) and an astonishing capacity to draw on reserves of skill and courage when pressed to the uttermost.

Some hint of the determination Moss was going to put into this race was shown in practice, always a hectic and strongly-disputed business at Monte Carlo where the grid position can mean so much. In spite of the tremendous showing of all the Ferraris, Moss took out his deep blue Lotus and knocked fractions of seconds off their times and also off the times of the more recent works Lotuses.

On the starting grid on the promenade of Monte Carlo harbour, the most colourful and exciting setting of any Grand Prix, was Moss in pole position, his car stripped of much of its side panelling to save a few pounds. Alongside him was Ginther's latest Ferrari, and beyond the Ferrari the very fast works Lotus of Jim Clark. The 120-degree V6 Ferrari engine startlingly demonstrated its potential, leaping away for the gasworks hairpin in first place, with Moss in hot pursuit, as Louis Chiron dropped the flag.

Up the hill towards the Casino tore the little low machines in quivering line-ahead, disappearing towards the hazards of the square, then the station descent through tortuous corners, and the curving dark tunnel that strains drivers' eyes to the utmost. It took Ginther just 108.4 seconds to accomplish his first 1.9-mile lap, Clark now brushing his tail, then Moss, and Tony Brooks in the first of the B.R.M.'s. On the next lap with Clark already in the pits, Moss began an assault on the faster Ferrari of Ginther.

It was a typical Moss chase, relentless and fearful for the pursued. The less experienced American kept his nerve and fought back, making use of all his superior power. But still the gap closed, from six to five, from five to four seconds. Moss began to make intimidating darts, thrusting the nose of his Lotus up alongside the shark-like Ferrari on the braking point at the corners, to remind the American he was there — there all the time, ready to pounce! On the fourteenth lap he edged up on the inside before the hairpin, switched to the outside, almost grazing the outside kerb on the exit, came hard alongside the Ferrari — and was suddenly away, just as if the Ferrari had lost all its power. That was what it was like to be passed by the master!

The remainder of this long, thrilling race round the crowd-packed streets of the city was made up of a series of attacks by the Ferrari drivers, first Hill, then Ginther leading the offensive, while von Trips — always a menace until his engine roughened up — lay behind in support: three faster red cars against the lone Briton, pressing him harder and harder — so hard that Moss commented after it was all over, 'Every lap was a sprint!'

To see Moss, lap after lap, changing down and braking from around 100 m.p.h. to 20 m.p.h. for the hairpin, smoke rising from his tyres, his exposed feet pumping at the pedals, his hands darting for the gear lever, all with superb precision and speed, was an unforgettable sight.

Look at the final times to judge the tenseness of the last laps, after 194 miles of motor racing:

Stirling Moss   Lotus-Climax   2 hrs 45 mins 50.1 sec

Richie Ginther	Ferrari	2 hrs 45 mins 53.7 secs
Phil Hill	Ferrari	2 hrs 46 mins 31.4 secs
W. von Trips	Ferrari	two laps behind

And Moss's speed of 70.71 m.p.h. was an all-time record, faster than the 2½ litre cars of the last formula, faster than the supercharged 1 litre cars before them, faster by far than the 5 litre and 6 litre German monsters of the 1930's on the same circuit.

230.   *Was this his finest hour? Near the close of his remarkable racing career, Stirling Moss put on what many consider to be his greatest demonstration of Grand Prix driving, round the streets of Monte Carlo. He took the lead on the fourteenth lap from the new, faster Ferrari of Ginther, and with cool precision held it to the end. Here, with arms crossed, he takes Rob Walker's dark blue Lotus through the old station hairpin*

230

The Champion from Down Under

The scene is the Sebring circuit in December, 1959, a drab concrete old airfield, miles from anywhere, in Florida, U.S.A. Only about 20,000 Americans have come to witness the first-ever Grand Prix on United States soil. This is an opportunity wasted, for it is to be a great race, a World Championship decider, with all the European stars performing, including Stirling Moss and the full Ferrari team.

This is to be an historic race for other reasons, for it will be won by a twenty-one-year-old New Zealand driver, and it will give the World Championship for the first time to an Australian driver. The Championship is wide open this year. Stirling Moss, who has fought for so long and in vain for the title, Tony Brooks, or that stalwart Australian, Jack Brabham, are all contestants for the supreme motor racing award.

Moss has lapped fastest in his Cooper in practice, and gained pole position, but Brabham in a works Cooper has been only three seconds slower round the flat, winding circuit. Way back on the fourth row of the grid is Bruce McLaren — a mere novice in this tough world of Grand Prix motor racing, but a deter-

232

233

1959

231—233. First United States World Championship Grand Prix, Sebring. Above: the grid line-up, Moss (7), Brabham (8), Schell (19), all on Coopers. The Ferraris behind, already looking massive in contrast, are in the hands of Brooks (2) and von Trips (4). Centre and below Bruce McLaren, in the second works Cooper, holds second place behind the Australian. Brabham ran out of fuel half a mile from the flag, pushed his car home into fourth place — enough to make him World Champion

mined and skilful driver.

Moss goes away at the fall of the flag, and builds up a big lead over the Australian, while McLaren holds on hard behind: three Coopers hold the first three places. Moss has got to win and make the fastest lap to gain the Championship. And for a time it looks as though, at last, he is going to succeed.

Then once again the Moss jinx strikes. His gearbox fails — and he his next seen walking slowly back to the pits. Brabham now has a clear lead, with his fellow-driver from down under slipstreaming him. The race average is over 98 m.p.h. The Cooper is sounding as healthy as on the first lap. The chequered flag is

1960

234. *Bruce McLaren made a fine showing with the Cooper team in the 1960 season. Above: he came in second, less than a minute after Moss, at Monaco*

235. *He drove always with style and dash*

236. 237. Calm, imperturbable, and well-nigh uncatchable, Brabham demonstrated the fine balance of the Cooper, and the power of its 2½ litre Climax engine throughout the 1960 season, to score his second World Championship. Here (and opposite above) he is at Spa for the Belgian Grand Prix, which he won by a comfortable margin from team-mate McLaren

brought out and raised. The reception committee is ready for the new World Champion.

But on that last lap fate strikes a hard blow. Out of sight of the stands, the Cooper engine coughs and spits, cuts out, runs for a few more revs — and dies. Brabham pulls in to the side of the track, out of fuel. McLaren races ahead. 'Suddenly,' said young McLaren in surprise after it was all over, 'I found myself winning.'

The drama is not yet over. Brabham climbs out and begins pushing. For more than half a mile, under the burning Florida sun, he heaves at his car, and by a miraculous effort at last gets it over the line, to fall exhausted on the concrete beside it. He has finished, and that is good enough. He is World Champion after all!

Jack Brabham, the most successful and experienced of the drivers from Australia and New Zealand who have come to Europe, is now forty years old, and a veteran with more than a decade of experience in sports car and Grand Prix racing behind him — and nearly ten more years in his home country. This quiet, studious engineer-driver began his career on four fast-moving wheels amid the hurly-burly of midget car racing in Sydney. Like Stirling Moss, the late Peter Collins and so many others, he worked his racing apprenticeship in Cooper 500's. Later he installed an 1,100 c.c. engine in his car, and with this won the Redex Pointscore Trophy, his first major success. Next came a Formula II (2 litre) Cooper-Bristol, which served him so well for nearly two years, winning almost everything for which he entered, that he widened his ambitions and decided to try his hand in Britain.

That was in 1955, and during his first season, mainly in smaller events, he did not earn very much more than exclamatory remarks from those who watched him exercising his dirt-track inspired style — such as 'hang out the tail and hope for the best'. With the help of John Cooper — and these two were to have a long friendship as well as a fruitful racing association — he entered one of the new rear-engined Cooper sports cars, fitted with a bored-out Bristol engine, for the British Grand Prix — no less. Apart from the laughter this aroused, it was notable only for being by far the

slowest car on the Aintree circuit, and lasted barely thirty laps. However, Brabham did so much better later in the 1955 season, that he was encouraged to return to Europe the following year. This time, after unfortunate experiences with a Maserati, Brabham consolidated his relationship with the Cooper factory and ran their new Formula II (1½ litre) racing car, with more discretion and more success. There were one or two occasions — at Oulton Park for instance against Roy Salvadori — when real championship quality was discernible.

The year 1957 marked the beginning of Jack Brabham's maturity as a driver. Now he was with the official Cooper works team, and he started off sensationally at Monaco with a 2 litre car against the full 2½ litre works Ferraris, Maseratis, Vanwalls and others, and with Moss and Fangio at the top of their form.

Nobody quite saw how it happened, perhaps because the little rear-engined car was considered too insignificant to have a chance, but suddenly it became evident that he was running *third,* with but a few miles to go to the flag! This Jack-the-giant-killer act was halted only by some slight mechanical complaint, but by dint of tremendous pushing he still managed to gain sixth place.

There were further successes in Formula I and sports car events in 1958, including a magnificent shared victory with Moss in an Aston Martin at the Nurburgring 1,000 km. But in Grands Prix the Coopers remained underpowered and not too reliable, although Brabham made an almost clean sweep with the Formula II Cooper. He was still learning all the time — how to conserve the engine and tyres, how to play the waiting game when tactics called for this, and learning by off-the-circuit study of the subtleties of design of the Formula I Grand Prix car.

For 1959 John Cooper had decided to enter a full team of Grand Prix cars, using the new 2½ litre Coventry-Climax engine whenever possible. There have been earlier references in this book to the 'rear-engine revolution'. This was the year when it became fully established, mainly by the joint efforts of the Coopers

238

238. Cooper and Brabham supreme. During his Championship years, Jack Brabham appeared with apparent effortless ease and almost monotonous regularity at the head of the procession, in Britain, and all over Europe. Here he is at Brands Hatch during the Silver City Trophy race in 1960

1961

239. Back to down under — and Australian Jack Brabham notches up another victory in New Zealand

Racing in the Antipodes

240. 241. For many years now the Grand Prix 'circus' has come out from Europe to take part in Australian and New Zealand events. Above and below: Moss in the hundreds; temperature was 106.9 degrees in the 1961 Warwick Farm 100-mile race near Sydney

1962

242. New Zealand Grand Prix. John Surtees (Ferrari) leads the way into the first corner. Rain was torrential — to the delight of Moss, who was in the lead when the race was abandoned after 100 miles

as designers and Brabham as number one driver; but not forgetting Bruce McLaren, the team's new recruit.

When Moss's car held together, the Australian was rarely able to compete with him; but careful preparation before a race and careful preservation of the machine during it are all part of the race-winning formula, and this was something that Brabham understood. He achieved his first victory at Monte Carlo after Moss fell out, ran second at Zandvoort, third on the exceedingly fast Rheims circuit, where no one could catch the Ferraris. At Aintree for the British Grand Prix, Brabham put up his greatest performance,

taking the lead at the start, and holding it undisputed to the end. This was the sort of demonstration that would be repeated many times in the future. Clutch trouble put him out of the German Grand Prix, and (rare event indeed) he crashed and injured himself, but only slightly, in the Portuguese event. Moss took the honours at Monza, and Brabham had to be content with a third, though this also sufficed to keep him at the head of the Championship. Then there was an agonizing nine-week wait before the deciding round at Sebring — which ended in the Australian's favour.

In 1960 the works Coopers were almost unbeatable. Rarely has there been a season in which one make

240

241

has been so omnipotent. And never have drivers from Australia and New Zealand so dominated the world of Grand Prix racing. Bruce McLaren as number two Cooper driver won magnificently in the Argentine, and took second place at Monaco less than a minute behind Moss. Then Brabham took over the star role, winning no less than five Championship events in a row — though in all fairness the story might have been different had not Moss seriously injured himself at Spa. Gone now was every hint of the young dirt racer style of five years earlier. Brabham drove with the cool, studied precision of a Farina or a Moss. Off the track he was reserved (no drinking, no smoking),

preoccupied, but friendly and ready to smile. In temperament he was about as far removed as he could be from, say, the fiery Nuvolari of the 1930's or the ebullient Mike Hawthorn, the previous holder of the Championship. But around the circuits of Europe no one was better liked.

Since 1960 Brabham has given more of his time to engineering and design work, and has set up a garage and works of his own. He began building his own cars, powered by Coventry-Climax, and by 1963 these Brabhams were going very fast, in the hands of the American Dan Gurney and Brabham himself, taking third place behind Lotus and B.R.M. — and ahead

1963

243. New Zealand's greatest driver, Bruce McLaren, remained loyal to Cooper. A very fast, very steady Grand Prix conductor, he took third place in the Belgian Grand Prix on the Spa-Francorchamps circuit

244. He took fifth place at Monaco, here sandwiched between Lorenzo Bandini's Ferrari and the Lotus of Australian driver Paul Hawkins

245. Australian and New Zealand drivers have made a great mark on the Grand Prix scene in the last decade. Here are three of the finest, veteran Jack Brabham

246. Bruce McLaren

247. Denis Hulme

of Ferrari — in the Constructors' Championship.

Jack Brabham still drives, and drives fast with all his old smooth unflurried style. But now that he is forty he is more ready to give up his cockpit to younger drivers. His mark on post-war motor racing has been made, and it is not possible to overestimate it. At Indianapolis and in Europe it was he who demonstrated for the first time, in practical terms, the significance of the new design principles set out by the Coopers. Today others are coming up from down under to take his place — Frank Gardner from Australia, and Denis Hulme from New Zealand, for example — and everyone is glad to know that there will be Aussies and Kiwis on the starting grids for many years to come.

Watch this Race!

Come for a moment to the mountainous Auvergne country in central France to watch a race that linked the greatest of the old with the greatest of the new. In 1905, before the first-ever Grand Prix, a 341-mile race was run through the Auvergne mountains. 'To describe the circuit in detail,' wrote a contemporary reporter, 'would be something like detailing a "looping the loop" performance. It is all turning and twisting, climbing up and going down.' This was the last of the Gordon Bennett series, and a terrific affair it was, with tremendous cars in the hands of muscular drivers — the machines and the men described in the first chapter of this book. The winner of this dusty, tortuous epic was Théry in a Brasier at a speed of over 48 m.p.h. (Try the same circuit today and see if you can average 30 m.p.h!)

To celebrate the sixtieth anniversary of this great race, the Automobile Club d'Auvergne was invited to organize France's senior event in 1965. This club, one of the most enterprising in France, had over the years run numerous races over their own special circuit in the Auvergne hills outside Clermont-Ferrand. But not since that last Gordon Bennett Cup event had the French Grand Prix come to the Auvergne. And that is a pity, for it is the most exciting and beautiful circuit in France — five miles long, fifty-one corners, three hairpins, and a difference in height of over 600 feet from the lowest valley to the highest hill.

This was the last year of the $1\frac{1}{2}$ litre Formula I. Most of the cars were at the height of their development; their drivers understood them and had driven them faster round the circuits of Europe than any earlier Grand Prix cars, in spite of their diminutive engines. But few of the drivers knew this circuit, so that the practice periods were vitally important. During the last session, on a misty, damp afternoon that made the circuit especially treacherous, newcomer Jackie Stewart broke all records in his B.R.M., and looked all set for pole position when the imperturbable Jim Clark, the fastest driver anywhere in the world, went out for the last time in his Lotus, and knocked off a few fractions of a second from Stewart's time.

This was one of the most tightly competitive fields ever seen on a Grand Prix grid, and it seemed as if all the constructors had developed the roadholding and engine output of their machines to the final degree of perfection. There were four different makes — Lotus, B.R.M., Ferrari and Brabham — among the first five on the two front rows. Technically the most fascinating was the Japanese Honda, powered by a V12 engine installed transversely behind the driver and inclined at a forward angle. It was the only car still liable to teething troubles, but in the hands of Richie Ginther lapped only 3.1 seconds slower than Clark's Lotus. In fact there was a difference of only five seconds between the first ten cars. So, above all, this was going to be a driver's race — and who could match the peerless Clark, fresh from his triumph at Indianapolis? Perhaps Graham Hill, ex-World Champion; perhaps John Surtees, reigning champion and leading Ferrari driver.

The damp, sultry morning had given way to blazing sun. The Prime Minister of France had made a lap of honour before the crowd of a quarter of a million who packed the enclosures and stands. The curtain-raiser Formula III race had been run. And soon after 2.30 p.m., a cloud of blue smoke and the howl of seventeen Grand Prix engines arose from the short straight in front of the pits.

M. Jacques Loste of the A.C.F. raised the flag, and as it swept down the pack tore away for the first sharp left-hander less than a hundred yards away. They streamed through, Clark with a white dust mask across his face — reminiscent of those Gordon Bennett drivers of so long ago — on the inside and already in the lead. Then Stewart, hard behind him, then Bandini's red Ferrari, and the remainder in a bunch. Bandini had the newer flat-twelve machine and for a while it seemed as if he might catch the flying Scotsman. Gurney came up to third, Surtees tailing him closely. The squat white Honda, with Ginther working hard, was going very fast; this car would surely be

1965

248. To celebrate the fiftieth anniversary of the 1905 Gordon Bennett race run among the Auvergne mountains, the French Grand Prix was held on the winding race circuit outside Clermont-Ferrand for the first time. Here is the tumultuous start — Jim Clark already leading the sixteen other cars

249. The first bend of the 1965 French Grand Prix. Clark's Lotus leads Bandini's red Ferrari, closely followed by Stewart. The newly tested Honda is lying in sixth position with Ginther in the cockpit

a race-winner one day.

In less than a minute they were up to the highest point of the circuit with its marvellous panoramic view across the plain to the north, and then they began the winding descent, much of the way with a steep drop on the outside that deterred over-excited drivers from overtaking.

They raced down to the hairpin on the valley floor in one long, sun-drenched, colourful line. Clark had pulled out a lead of a dozen yards, the way he has always preferred — get clear away in the first dozen or so laps, and hold it like that to the end. And it is remarkable how often he manages to do just this.

Then steeply up through sharp climbing turns like fighter-pilots battling for altitude, the fat tyres of these strange little whippy four-wheel velocipedes edging over the white verge line and grazing the straw bales. How Nazzaro and Werner, Jenatzy and Earp and the rest of those heroes of the Gordon Bennett Cup would have relished this scene! Though perhaps they might have thought these miniatures were no machines for really tough racing drivers!

Jackie Stewart was showing great form. He hadn't Clark's polish, nor his steadiness of line round the corners, but he was drawing every ounce of power from his B.R.M. and going very fast. He sailed past Bandini on the second lap, to set about Clark. But Clark had seen the danger, knocked a second off his next lap, and held off the B.R.M. assault. Then Gurney, too, took his Brabham past the Italian, and finally Surtees got past his team-mate. At the end of the third lap it was Lotus, B.R.M., Brabham, Ferrari, Ferrari. Bucknum couldn't find enough sparks to keep his Honda going, and once again the Japanese car made an early retirement. Five laps later Ginther brought his Honda in for the last time to its pit.

Clark was still putting on the pressure, lapping at close to 90 m.p.h., hoping for despair or repair among those who might threaten him. Stewart never lost heart. But those who were farther behind were falling out one by one — the veteran Jo Bonnier, Gurney,

250. *Fifty-one corners on every lap — forty laps in all. This is half way round the first lap, with 'Farmer' Clark already well away from the opposition. The mask is to protect his face from stones, which were like pebbles on Brighton beach on some of the corners*

250

Innes Ireland with a jammed gearbox. The frailty of these cars would have amazed those old Gordon Bennett racers! Seven cars were out by half time. But the leading Lotus and B.R.M. were going great guns and sounded as if they could last a day. Every few laps Clark knocked a little off the lap record, just to show what he had in hand.

Down deep in the valley there was a minor shunt when one driver spun around, and another knocked into him, losing a wheel. But most of the driving was faultless, a superb demonstration on a wonderful circuit of how extremely professional the real professionals are in Grand Prix racing today. Even Graham Hill, with neck in a rubber support after an accident the previous year, was showing what style really is; though his handicap prevented him from getting among the leaders, and Clark lapped him before the end.

Jackie Stewart made one last effort to close the gap, but this was by now too wide. Only a mistake from Clark could give him the lead, and that sort of error just didn't happen. Surtees was still going very fast in third place, his engine stuttering so badly in spite of one quick pit stop that one wondered if Clark could have sailed so clear away if the V8 Ferrari engine had been sparking properly.

After $2\frac{1}{4}$ hours racing Clark swept round those fifty-one corners for the last time, made his last couple of hundred or so gear changes, and tore past the chequered flag a half minute ahead of the B.R.M. Stewart had driven so superbly from the start.

And thus ended in this beautiful setting the 51st Grand Prix of the Automobile Club de France — in a blaze of glory for Britain, in the land that began this magnificent business of motor racing, once dominated it, but now alas! seems to have lost all interest.

252. *John Surtees, now as famous on four wheels as he used to be on two, drove an impeccable race for Ferrari; but the Italian car could not match the Lotus's cornering*

253. It had all looked so easy! Jim Clark had not put a wheel
wrong from start to finish — it was polished, supremely fast
driving of the highest quality

253

Acknowledgements

Alfa Romeo, Milan: pages 70 (top and centre), 93 (bottom).

"Autocar", London: pages 11 (bottom), 12 (top and bottom), 16, 17, 18, 19, 20, 21, 22, 24 (left), 27, 28 (upper centre, lower centre and bottom), 31 (top), 40, 42, 43, 44, 45, 47 (bottom left and bottom right), 99 (bottom), 101 (bottom), 120 (centre and bottom), 121, 122, 123 (bottom), 129 (bottom)

J. Maxwell Boyd, London: pages 126 (bottom)126—127, 128 (top).

British Petroleum Co. Ltd., London: pages 140, 143, 147 (top).

Central Press Photos Ltd., London: pages 83 (top and centre), 84, 107 (top right), 108, 112 (top), 113 (bottom), 119 (top and centre) 137 (bottom left and bottom right), 138 (top and bottom), 138—139, 141 (top right and bottom right).

Citroen, Paris: page 7 (top and bottom).

H. G. Conway, London: pages 26 (top), 46 (centre), 48 (top left and top right), 49 (top), 69 (bottom).

Daimler-Benz AG, Stuttgart-Untertürkheim: pages 10 (top and centre left), 11 (top right), 14, 15 (bottom), 30, 71 (bottom left), 72, 73, 80, 90, 91 92, 93 (top), 94—95, 96, 102, 104 (bottom), 117.

Fiat, Turin: pages 23 (top), 41 (top), 46 (top and bottom), 47 (top), 49 (bottom).

Geoffrey Goddard, London: frontispiece, pages 104 (top left and top right), 105, 115, 116 (bottom), 119 (bottom), 124 (top), 126 (top), 128 (bottom), 131 (bottom left and bottom right), 136, 137 (top), 144—145.

Guy Griffiths, Thames Ditton, Surrey: page 100.

Paul Hamlyn Library: pages 15 (top), 41 (bottom right).

Richard Hough, London: page 29 (bottom).

Indianapolis Motor Speedway Corporation, U.S.A.: pages 32 (bottom), 33, 34 (top, centre and bottom), 35 (bottom), 50, 51, 52, 53, 54, 55, 63 (bottom left), 99 (top), 101 (top).

Keystone Press Agency Ltd., London: pages 109 (top), 111 (bottom).

Louis Klemantaski, London: pages 65, 66—67, 68, 69 (top), 70 (bottom), 74 (top), 75 (bottom), 76, 77, 78, 79, 85, 86—87, 88, 89 (top), 103, 106—107(top and bottom), 109 (bottom), 110, 111 (top), 112 (centre), 114, 116(top left), 118, 120 (top), 125, 129 (top), 131 (top), 132—133, 135.

Max Le Grand, Dartford, Kent: page 116 (top right).

London Express News and Feature Services, London: page 2.

Montagu Motor Museum, Beaulieu, Hants: pages 10 (centre right), 11 (top left), 13 (top), 31 (bottom), 39.

"Motor", London: Binding, pages 83 (bottom), 123 (top).

"Motor Sport", London: pages 124 (bottom), 130, 134.

D. Napier and Son Ltd., London: page 23 (bottom).

Petersen Publishing Company, Los Angeles, California, U.S.A.: pages 56, 57, 58, 59, 60, 61, 62, 63 (top left, top right, centre and bottom right), 64, 141 (top left).

David Phipps, Dartford, Kent: pages 146, 147 (bottom), 148—149.

Charles Pocklington, London: pages 112 (bottom), 113 (top).

Richard Poe, Longboat Key, Florida, U. S. A.: pages 97, 98.

Porsche, Stuttgart-Zuffenhausen: pages 71 (top and bottom right), 74 (bottom), 75 (top), 81, 89 (bottom).

Radio Times Hulton Picture Library, London: pages 8—9, 12 (centre), 28 (top), 35 (top), 36—37, 38.

Renault Ltd., London: pages 13 (bottom), 32 (top).

Société des Automobiles Peugeot, Paris: pages 24—25, 41 (bottom left).

Vauxhall Motors Ltd., Luton: pages 26 (bottom), 29 (top).

Index